Python Data Mining
Quick Start Guide

A beginner's guide to extracting valuable insights
from your data

Nathan Greeneltch

BIRMINGHAM - MUMBAI

Python Data Mining Quick Start Guide

Commissioning Editor: Amey Varangaonkar
Acquisition Editor: Reshma Raman
Content Development Editor: Smit Carvalho
Technical Editor: Diksha Wakode
Copy Editor: Safis Editing
Project Coordinator: Kinjal Bari
Proofreader: Safis Editing
Indexer: Pratik Shirodkar
Graphics: Alishon Mendonsa
Production Coordinator: Jayalaxmi Raja

First published: April 2019

Production reference: 1240419

Published by Packt Publishing Ltd.
Livery Place
35 Livery Street
Birmingham
B3 2PB, UK.

ISBN 978-1-78980-026-5

www.packtpub.com

To my children, Vaughn and Vera. They are the lit candle around every corner I turn.

`mapt.io`

Mapt is an online digital library that gives you full access to over 5,000 books and videos, as well as industry leading tools to help you plan your personal development and advance your career. For more information, please visit our website.

Why subscribe?

- Spend less time learning and more time coding with practical eBooks and Videos from over 4,000 industry professionals

- Improve your learning with Skill Plans built especially for you

- Get a free eBook or video every month

- Mapt is fully searchable

- Copy and paste, print, and bookmark content

Packt.com

Did you know that Packt offers eBook versions of every book published, with PDF and ePub files available? You can upgrade to the eBook version at `www.packt.com` and as a print book customer, you are entitled to a discount on the eBook copy. Get in touch with us at `customercare@packtpub.com` for more details.

At `www.packt.com`, you can also read a collection of free technical articles, sign up for a range of free newsletters, and receive exclusive discounts and offers on Packt books and eBooks.

Contributors

About the author

Nathan Greeneltch, PhD is a ML engineer at Intel Corp and resident data mining and analytics expert in the AI consulting group. He's worked with Python analytics in both the start-up realm and the large-scale manufacturing sector over the course of the last decade. Nathan regularly mentors new hires and engineers fresh to the field of analytics, with impromptu chalk talks and division-wide knowledge-sharing sessions at Intel. In his past life, he was a physical chemist studying surface enhancement of the vibration signals of small molecules; a topic on which he wrote a doctoral thesis while at Northwestern University in Evanston, IL. Nathan hails from the southeastern United States, with family in equal parts from Arkansas and Florida.

> *I'd like to thank my loving wife, Lei-Ann, who encouraged me from conception to completion of this book. It would not have been written without her. Also, I'd like to thank the students and colleagues that contributed to the narrative style and teaching methods I've adopted over the years. The list is long, but to name a few: Martin, Michael, Liu, Nan, Preethi, and Britt. Lastly, thank you to my family for supporting me and injecting the perspective that I share in this book.*

About the reviewer

Julian Quick is a graduate student attending the University of Colorado Boulder, studying turbulent flow modeling. Julian is interested in the optimization and uncertainty quantification of wind energy systems.

I would like to thank my advisors, Peter Hamlington and Ryan King, for their continued patience and encouragement.

Packt is searching for authors like you

If you're interested in becoming an author for Packt, please visit `authors.packtpub.com` and apply today. We have worked with thousands of developers and tech professionals, just like you, to help them share their insight with the global tech community. You can make a general application, apply for a specific hot topic that we are recruiting an author for, or submit your own idea.

Table of Contents

Preface   1

Chapter 1: Data Mining and Getting Started with Python Tools   7
  Descriptive, predictive, and prescriptive analytics   9
  What will and will not be covered in this book   10
    Recommended readings for further explanation   10
  Setting up Python environments for data mining   11
  Installing the Anaconda distribution and Conda package manager   12
    Installing on Linux   12
    Installing on Windows   13
    Installing on macOS   13
  Launching the Spyder IDE   13
  Launching a Jupyter Notebook   15
  Installing high-performance Python distribution   17
  Recommended libraries and how to install   18
    Recommended libraries   19
  Summary   20

Chapter 2: Basic Terminology and Our End-to-End Example   21
  Basic data terminology   21
    Sample spaces   22
    Variable types   22
    Data types   23
  Basic summary statistics   24
  An end-to-end example of data mining in Python   25
    Loading data into memory – viewing and managing with ease using pandas   25
    Plotting and exploring data – harnessing the power of Seaborn   26
    Transforming data – PCA and LDA with scikit-learn   30
    Quantifying separations – k-means clustering and the silhouette score   35
    Making decisions or predictions   36
  Summary   39

Chapter 3: Collecting, Exploring, and Visualizing Data   41
  Types of data sources and loading into pandas   41
    Databases   42
      Basic Structured Query Language (SQL) queries   43
    Disks   46
    Web sources   46
      From URLs   47
      From Scikit-learn and Seaborn-included sets   47

Access, search, and sanity checks with pandas   47
Basic plotting in Seaborn   53
Popular types of plots for visualizing data   53
   Scatter plots   54
   Histograms   56
   Jointplots   58
   Violin plots   59
   Pairplots   61
Summary   63

Chapter 4: Cleaning and Readying Data for Analysis   65
The scikit-learn transformer API   65
Cleaning input data   67
   Missing values   67
     Finding and removing missing values   68
     Imputing to replace the missing values   70
   Feature scaling   71
     Normalization   72
     Standardization   73
   Handling categorical data   74
     Ordinal encoding   74
     One-hot encoding   76
     Label encoding   78
High-dimensional data   79
Dimension reduction   79
   Feature selection   79
     Feature filtering   80
       The variance threshold   80
       The correlation coefficient   82
     Wrapper methods   84
       Sequential feature selection   84
   Transformation   86
     PCA   87
     LDA   89
Summary   91

Chapter 5: Grouping and Clustering Data   93
Introducing clustering concepts   94
   Location of the group   96
     Euclidean space (centroids)   96
     Non-Euclidean space (medioids)   97
   Similarity   97
     Euclidean space   98
       The Euclidean distance   98
       The Manhattan distance   98
       Maximum distance   99
     Non-Euclidean space   99
       The cosine distance   100

The Jaccard distance | 100
Termination condition | 100
With known number of groupings | 101
Without known number of groupings | 101
Quality score and silhouette score | 101
Clustering methods | 102
Means separation | 105
K-means | 106
Finding k | 107
K-means++ | 108
Mini batch K-means | 109
Hierarchical clustering | 109
Reuse the dendrogram to find number of clusters | 113
Plot dendrogram | 114
Density clustering | 114
Spectral clustering | 116
Summary | 119

Chapter 6: Prediction with Regression and Classification | 121
Scikit-learn Estimator API | 121
Introducing prediction concepts | 122
Prediction nomenclature | 124
Mathematical machinery | 125
Loss function | 125
Gradient descent | 127
Fit quality regimes | 131
Regression | 132
Metrics of regression model prediction | 132
Regression example dataset | 133
Linear regression | 134
Extension to multivariate form | 135
Regularization with penalized regression | 136
Regularization penalties | 137
Classification | 139
Classification example dataset | 140
Metrics of classification model prediction | 141
Multi-class classification | 141
One-versus-all | 142
One-versus-one | 142
Logistic regression | 143
Regularized logistic regression | 146
Support vector machines | 146
Soft-margin with C | 150
The kernel trick | 150
Tree-based classification | 151
Decision trees | 152
Node splitting with Gini | 153
Random forest | 154

Avoid overfitting and speed up the fits   155
Built-in validation with bagging   155
Tuning a prediction model   157
Cross-validation   157
Introduction of the validation set   158
Multiple validation sets with k-fold method   159
Grid search for hyperparameter tuning   160
Summary   161
Chapter 7: Advanced Topics - Building a Data Processing Pipeline and Deploying It   163
Pipelining your analysis   163
Scikit-learn's pipeline object   164
Deploying the model   166
Serializing a model and storing with the pickle module   167
Loading a serialized model and predicting   167
Python-specific deployment concerns   167
Summary   168
Other Books You May Enjoy   169
Index   173

Preface

This book introduces data mining with popular free Python libraries. It is written in a conversational style, aiming to be approachable while imparting intuition on the reader. Data mining is a broad field of analytical methods designed to uncover insights from your data that are not obvious or discoverable by conventional analysis techniques. The field of data mining is vast, so the topics in this quick start guide were chosen by their relevance to not only their field of origin, but also the adjacent applications of machine learning and artificial intelligence. After a procedural first half, focused on getting the reader comfortable with data collection, loading, and munging, the book will move to a completely conceptual discussion. The concepts are introduced from first principles intuition and broadly grouped as transformation, clustering, and prediction. Popular methods such as principal component analysis, k-means clustering, support vector machines, and random forest are all covered in the conceptual second half of the book. The book ends with a discussion on pipe-lining and deploying your analytical models.

Who this book is for

This book is targeted at individuals who are new to the field or data mining and analytics with Python. Very little background is assumed in Python programming or math above the high-school level. All of the Python libraries used in the book are freely available at no cost on a variety of platforms, so anyone with access to the internet should be able to learn and practice the concepts introduced.

What this book covers

The first three and a half chapters of the book are focused on the procedural nuts and bolts of a data mining project. This includes creating a data mining Python environment, loading data from a variety of sources, and munging the data for downstream analysis. The remaining content in the book is mostly conceptual, and delivered in a conversational style very close to how I would train a new hire at my company.

`Chapter 1`, *Data Mining and Getting Started with Python Tools*, covers the topic of getting started with your software environment. It also covers how to download and install high-speed Python and popular libraries such as `pandas`, `scikit-learn`, and `seaborn`. After reading this chapter and setting up your environment, you should be ready to follow along with the demonstrations throughout the rest of the book.

Chapter 2, *Basic Terminology and our End-to-End Example*, covers the basic statistics and data terminology that are required for working in data mining. The final portion of the chapter is dedicated to a full working example, which combined the types of techniques that will be introduced later on in this book. You will also have a better understanding of the thought processes behind analysis and the common steps taken to address a problem statement that you may encounter in the field.

Chapter 3, *Collecting, Exploring, and Visualizing Data*, covers the basics of loading data from databases, disks, and web sources. It also covers the basic SQL queries, and pandas' access and search functions. The last sections of the chapter introduce the common types of plots using Seaborn.

Chapter 4, *Cleaning and Readying Data for Analysis*, covers the basics of data cleanup and dimensionality reduction. After reading it, you will understand how to work with missing values, rescale input data, and handle categorical variables. You will also understand the troubles of high-dimensional data, and how to combat this with feature reduction techniques including filter, wrapper, and transformation methods.

Chapter 5, *Grouping and Clustering Data*, introduces the background and thought processes that goes into designing a clustering algorithm for data mining work. It then introduces common clustering methods in the field and carries out a comparison between all of them with toy datasets. After reading this chapter, you will know the difference between algorithms that cluster based on means separation, density, and connectivity. You will also be able to look at a plot of incoming data and have some intuition on whether clustering will fit your mining project.

Chapter 6, *Prediction with Regression and Classification*, covers the basics behind using a computer to learn prediction models by introducing the loss function and gradient descent. It then introduces the concepts of overfitting, underfitting, and the penalty approach to regularize your model during fits. It also covers common regression and classification techniques, and the regularized versions of each of these where appropriate. The chapter finishes with a discussion of best practices for model tuning, including cross-validation and grid search.

Chapter 7, *Advanced Topics – Building a Data Processing Pipeline and Deploying*, This chapter covers a strategy for pipe-lining and deploying using built-in Scikit-learn methods. It also introduces the `pickle` module for model persistence and storage, as well as discussing Python-specific concerns at deployment time.

To get the most out of this book

You should have basic understanding of the mathematical principles taught in American primary and high schools. The most complex math required is the understanding of the contents of a matrix and the relation implied by the sigma (sum) symbol. You should have some rudimentary knowledge of Python, including lists, dictionaries, and functions. If you feel deficient in any of these prerequisites, a quick internet search to brush up on the concepts prior to reading should get you ready quickly.

This book is meant as a beginner's text, so the most important prerequisite is an open mind and the drive to learn.

Download the example code files

You can download the example code files for this book from your account at www.packt.com. If you purchased this book elsewhere, you can visit www.packt.com/support and register to have the files emailed directly to you.

You can download the code files by following these steps:

1. Log in or register at www.packt.com.
2. Select the **SUPPORT** tab.
3. Click on **Code Downloads & Errata**.
4. Enter the name of the book in the **Search** box and follow the onscreen instructions.

Once the file is downloaded, please make sure that you unzip or extract the folder using the latest version of:

- WinRAR/7-Zip for Windows
- Zipeg/iZip/UnRarX for Mac
- 7-Zip/PeaZip for Linux

The code bundle for the book is also hosted on GitHub at https://github.com/PacktPublishing/Python-Data-Mining-Quick-Start-Guide. In case there's an update to the code, it will be updated on the existing GitHub repository.

We also have other code bundles from our rich catalog of books and videos available at https://github.com/PacktPublishing/. Check them out!

Download the color images

We also provide a PDF file that has color images of the screenshots/diagrams used in this book. You can download it here: https://www.packtpub.com/sites/default/files/downloads/9781789800265_ColorImages.pdf.

Conventions used

There are a number of text conventions used throughout this book:

A block of code is set as follows, with # used for comment lines:

```
from sklearn.cluster import Method
clus = Method(args*)
# fit to input data
clus.fit(X_input)
# get cluster assignments of X_input
X_assigned = clus.labels_
```

Any command-line input or output is written as follows:

```
(base) $ spyder
```

Bold: Indicates a new term, an important word, or words that you see onscreen. For example, words in menus or dialog boxes appear in the text like this. Here is an example: "Select **System info** from the **Administration** panel."

Warnings or important notes appear like this.

Tips and tricks appear like this.

Get in touch

Feedback from our readers is always welcome.

General feedback: If you have questions about any aspect of this book, mention the book title in the subject of your message and email us at `customercare@packtpub.com`.

Errata: Although we have taken every care to ensure the accuracy of our content, mistakes do happen. If you have found a mistake in this book, we would be grateful if you would report this to us. Please visit `www.packt.com/submit-errata`, selecting your book, clicking on the Errata Submission Form link, and entering the details.

Piracy: If you come across any illegal copies of our works in any form on the Internet, we would be grateful if you would provide us with the location address or website name. Please contact us at `copyright@packt.com` with a link to the material.

If you are interested in becoming an author: If there is a topic that you have expertise in and you are interested in either writing or contributing to a book, please visit `authors.packtpub.com`.

Reviews

Please leave a review. Once you have read and used this book, why not leave a review on the site that you purchased it from? Potential readers can then see and use your unbiased opinion to make purchase decisions, we at Packt can understand what you think about our products, and our authors can see your feedback on their book. Thank you!

For more information about Packt, please visit `packt.com`.

Data Mining and Getting Started with Python Tools

In a sense, data mining is a necessary and predictable response to the dawn of the information age. Indeed, every piece of the modern global economy relies more each year on information and an immense in-stream of data. The path from information pool to actionable insights has many steps. Data mining is typically defined as the pattern and/or trend discovery phase in the pipeline.

This book is a quick-start guide for data mining and will include utilitarian descriptions of the most important and widely used methods, including the mainstays among data professionals such as k-means clustering, random forest prediction, and principal component dimensionality reduction. Along the way, I will give you tips I've learned and introduce helpful scripting tools to make your life easier. Not only will I introduce the tools, but I will clearly describe what makes them so helpful and why you should take the time to learn them.

The first half of the book will cover the nuts and bolts of data collection and preparation. The second half will be more conceptual and will introduce the topics of transformation, clustering, and prediction. The conceptual discussions start in the middle of `Chapter 4`, *Cleaning and Readying Data for Analysis*, and are written solely as a conversation between myself and the reader. These conversations are ported mostly from the many adhoc training sessions I've done over the years on Intel office marker boards. The last chapter of the book will be on the deployment of these models. This topic is the natural next step for new practitioners and I will provide an introduction and references for when you think you are ready to take the next steps.

The following topics will be covered in this chapter:

- Descriptive, predictive, and prescriptive analytics
- What will and will not be covered in this book
- Setting up Python environments for data mining
- Installing the Anaconda distribution and Conda package manager
- Launching the Spyder IDE
- Launching a Jupyter Notebook
- Installing a high performance Python distribution
- Recommended libraries and how to install

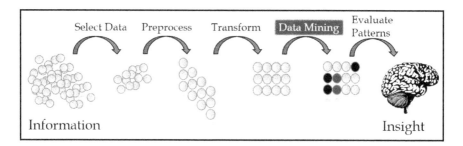

Practitioners should be familiar with the previous data selection, preprocessing, and transformation steps as well as the subsequent pattern and trend evaluation. Knowledge of the full process and an understanding of the goals will orient your data mining efforts in space and keep you aligned with the overall goal.

Descriptive, predictive, and prescriptive analytics

Practitioners in the field of data analysis usually break down their work into three genres of analytics, given as follows:

- **Descriptive**: Descriptive is the oldest field of analytics study and involves digging deep into the data to hunt down and extract previously unidentified trends, groupings, or other patterns. This was the predominant type of analytics done by the pioneering groups in the field of data mining, and for a number of years the two terms were considered more or less to mean the same thing. However, predictive analytics blossomed in the early 2000s along with the burgeoning field of machine learning, and the many of the techniques that came out of the data mining community proved useful for prediction.

- **Predictive**: Predictive analytics, as the name suggests, focuses on predicting future outcomes and relies on the assumption that past descriptions necessarily lead to future behavior. This concept demonstrates the strong and unavoidable connection between descriptive and predictive analytics. In recent years, industry has naturally taken the next logical step of using prediction to feed into prescriptive solutions.

- **Prescriptive**: Prescriptive analytics relies heavily on customer goals, seeks personalized scoring systems for predictions, and is still a relatively immature field of study and practice. This is accomplished by modeling various response strategies and scoring against the personalized score system.

Please see the following table for a summary:

Type of analytics	Problem statement addressed
Descriptive	What happened?
Predictive	What will happen next?
Prescriptive	How should we respond?

What will and will not be covered in this book

A quick and dirty description of data mining I hear in the field can be paraphrased as: "Descriptive and predictive analytics with a focus on previously hidden relationships or trends". As such, this book will cover these topics and skip the predictive analytics that focus on automation of obvious prediction, along with the entire field of prescriptive analytics entirely. This text is meant to be a quick start guide, so even the relevant fields of study will only be skimmed over and summarized. Please see the *Recommended reading for further explanation* section for inquiring minds that want to delve deeper into some of the subjects covered in this book.

Preprocessing and data transformation are typically considered to be outside of the data mining category. One of the goals of this book is to provide full working data mining examples, and basic preprocessing is required to do this right. So, this book will cover those topics, before delving in to the more traditional mining strategies.

 Throughout this book, I will throw in tips I've learned along my career journey around how to apply data mining to solve real-world problems. I will denote them in a special tip box like this one.

Recommended readings for further explanation

These books are good for more in-depth discussions and as an introduction to important and relevant topics. I recommend that you start with these if you want to become an expert:

- Data mining in practice:

  Data Mining: Practical Machine Learning Tools and Techniques, 4th Edition by Ian H. Witten (author), Eibe Frank (author), Mark A. Hall (author), Christopher J. Pal

- Data mining advanced discussion and mathematical foundation:

  Data Mining and Analysis: Fundamental Concepts and Algorithms, 1st Edition by Mohammed J. Zaki (author), Wagner Meira Jr (author)

- Computer science taught with Python:

  Python Programming: An Introduction to Computer Science, 3rd Edition by John Zelle (author)

- Python machine learning and analytics:

  Python Machine Learning: Machine Learning and Deep Learning with Python, scikit-learn, and TensorFlow, 2nd Edition Paperback—September 20, 2017 by Sebastian Raschka (author), Vahid Mirjalili (author)

  Advanced Machine Learning with Python Paperback—July 28, 2016 by John Hearty

Setting up Python environments for data mining

A computing setup conducive to advanced data mining requires a comfortable development environment and working libraries for data management, analytics, plotting, and deployment. The popular bundled Python distribution from Anaconda is a perfect fit for the job. It is targeted at scientists and engineers, and includes all the required packages to get started. Conda itself is a package manager for maintaining working Python environments and, of course, is included in the bundle. The package manager will allow you to install/remove combinations of libraries into segregated Python environments, all the while reconciling any version dependencies between the distinct libraries.

It includes an integrated development environment called **The Scientific Python Development Environment** (**Spyder**) and a ready-to-use implementation of Jupyter Notebook interface. Both of these development environments use the interactive Python console called IPython. IPython gives you a live console for scripting. You can run a single line of code, check results, then run another line of code in same console in an interactive fashion. A few trial-and-error sessions with IPython will demonstrate very clearly why these Python tools are so beloved by practitioners working in a rapid prototyping environment.

Installing the Anaconda distribution and Conda package manager

These tools from Anaconda are available on both Windows and Linux systems. See the following install instructions.

Installing on Linux

To install the distribution, follow these steps given as follows:

1. First, download the latest installer build from `https://www.anaconda.com/download/#linux`.

2. Then, in the Linux Terminal, pass this bash command:

```
$ bash Anaconda-latest-Linux-x86_64.sh
```

3. Follow the prompts in the terminal and it will begin installing. Once done, you will be asked if you want to allow Conda to be auto-initialized with a `.bashrc` entry. I recommend choosing `N` and activating it manually when needed, just in case you decide to have multiple versions of Conda on your system. In this case, you can launch the Conda prompt by using the following command:

```
$ source /{anaconda3_dir}/bin/activate
```

This is will source the Conda activate shell script and call it to activate the `base` environment, which is the default Anaconda Python bundle. Adding new environments will be discussed in the following section on how to install specific libraries. At this point, passing the Python command will open an interactive shell where you can execute Python code line-by-line, as shown in the following code snippet:

```
(base) $ Python
Python 3.7.0 (default, Jun 28 2018, 13:15:42)
[GCC 7.2.0] :: Anaconda, Inc. on linux
Type "help", "copyright", "credits" or "license" for more
information.
>>> import numpy
>>> numpy.random.random(10)
array([0.48489815, 0.80944492, 0.89740441, 0.93031125, 0.71774534,
       0.63817451, 0.93231809, 0.75820457, 0.17550135, 0.62126858])
```

Alternatively, you can execute the code in a stored Python script by using the following command:

```
(base) $ Python script.py
```

Installing on Windows

To install on Windows, follow the steps given as follows:

1. First, download the executable from `https://conda.io/docs/user-guide/install/windows.html`
2. Then, launch the Anaconda prompt that can be found in a program search from the Windows **Start** menu

Anaconda prompt is a Windows command prompt with all the environment variables set to point to Anaconda. That's it; you are ready to use your base Python environment.

Installing on macOS

To install on macOS, follow the steps given as follows:

1. First, download the graphical installer from the Anaconda distribution site `https://www.anaconda.com/distribution/`
2. Launch the package and follow the on-screen prompts, which should set up everything you need automatically

Launching the Spyder IDE

Spyder can be started by passing `spyder` into the Anaconda prompt as follows:

```
(base) $ spyder
```

As mentioned earlier, Spyder uses the IPython interactive console. So, you can pass code line-by-line directly into the console. See the following screenshot for two lines of Python code passed one at a time:

```
IPython console
  Console 1/A  X

Python 3.7.0 (default, Jun 28 2018, 13:15:42)
Type "copyright", "credits" or "license" for more information.

IPython 6.5.0 -- An enhanced Interactive Python.

In [1]: import numpy

In [2]: numpy.random.random(10)
Out[2]:
array([0.77427787, 0.78390182, 0.35564681, 0.49296041, 0.69766155,
       0.09072515, 0.04044033, 0.81377416, 0.90574834, 0.55837327])
```

Alternatively, you can edit a script in the editor and execute by pressing the green play button at the top of the IDE. This causes the script to be dumped into the IPython console, then run line-by-line:

```
File  Edit  Search  Source  Run  Debug  Consoles  Projects  Tools  View  Help

Editor - /home/nathan/.config/spyder-py3/temp.py
  temp.py  X

1 # -*- coding: utf-8 -*-
2 """
3 Spyder Editor
4
5 This is a temporary script file.
6 """
7
8 import numpy
9 numpy.random.random(10)
```

The interactive IPython console also can display images and plots inline in the same console window. This is yet another feature that is very convenient for interactive data mining and rapid prototyping of analytics models:

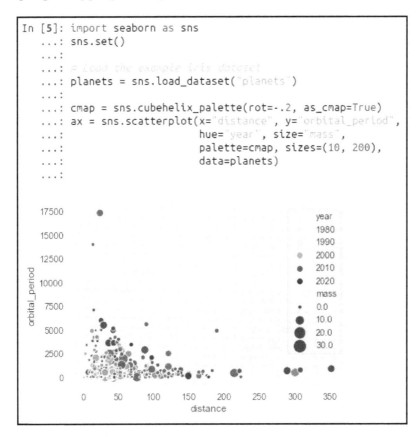

Launching a Jupyter Notebook

The Jupyter project spun out of the popular IPython Notebook work of the early 2000s. These notebooks provide a visual interface with sequential text and code cells. This allows you to add some text to describe a solution, then follow it with code examples. The Jupyter Notebook also use the IPython console (similar to Spyder), so you have an interactive code interpretor that can plot images inline. Launching the notebook from the Anaconda prompt is simple:

```
(base) $ jupyter notebook
```

The Jupyter project maintains a few basic notebooks. Let's look at a screenshot from one of them, as follows (it can be found at `http://nbviewer.jupyter.org/github/temporaer/tutorial_ml_gkbionics`):

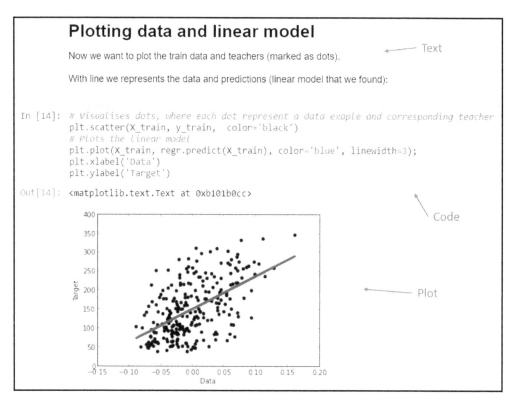

The concept is self-explanatory if we look at a few examples. The following are recommendations for some relevant and helpful Jupyter Notebooks on data mining and analytics from around the web:

`https://github.com/rasbt/python-machine-learning-book/blob/master/code/ch01/ch01.ipynb`

`http://nbviewer.jupyter.org/github/amplab/datascience-sp14/blob/master/hw2/HW2.ipynb`

`https://github.com/TomAugspurger/PyDataSeattle/blob/master/notebooks/1.%20Basics.ipynb`

Installing high-performance Python distribution

Intel Corp has built a bundle of Python libraries with accelerations for **High-Performance Computing** (**HPC**) on CPUs. The vast majority of the accelerations come with no code changes, because they are snuck in under the hood. All the concepts and libraries introduced in the rest of the book will run faster in the HPC Intel Python environment. Luckily, Intel has a Conda version of their distribution, so you can add it as a new Conda environment via the following few command lines in the Anaconda prompt:

```
(base) $ Conda create -n idp -c channel intelpython3_full Python=3
(base) $ Conda activate idp
```

Full disclosure: I work for Intel, so I won't focus too much on this HPC distribution. I will merely let the performance numbers speak for themselves. See the following graph for raw speedup numbers (optimized versus stock) when using unchanged Scikit-learn code on CPU:

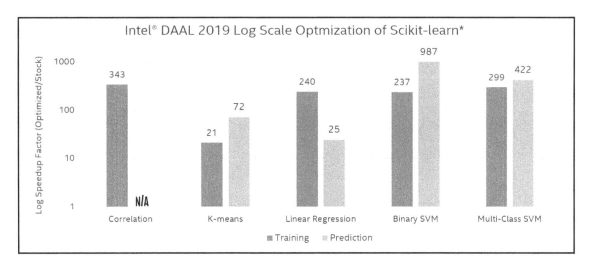

Recommended libraries and how to install

Its easy to add or remove libraries from the Anaconda prompt. Once you have an the preferred environment activated, the simple `Conda install` command will search the Anaconda cloud repo for a matching package, and will begin download if it exists. Conda will warn if there are version dependencies with your other libraries. Always pay attention to these warnings, so that you know if any other library versions are affected. If, at any time, you need a reminder of what is in your environment, use the `Conda list` command to check package names and versions.

Let's look at some example commands:

1. Create a new environment called `my_env` with Python version 3 using the following command:

   ```
   (base) $ Conda create -n my_env Python=3
   ```

2. Check whether `my_env` was created successfully by using the following command:

   ```
   (base) $ Conda info --envs
   ```

   You will see the following screen on the execution of the preceding command:

   ```
   (base) nathan@nathan-ThinkPad-Twist:~$ conda info --envs
   # conda environments:
   #
   base                  *  /home/nathan/anaconda3
   idp                      /home/nathan/anaconda3/envs/idp
   my_env                   /home/nathan/anaconda3/envs/my_env
   ```

3. Activate a new environment by using the following command:

   ```
   (base) $ Conda activate my_env
   ```

4. Install the `numpy` math library by using the following command:

   ```
   (my_env) $ Conda install numpy
   ```

5. Use `Conda list` as follows, to check whether a new library was installed or not and all other libraries and versions in `my_env`:

   ```
   (my_env) $ Conda list
   ```

You will see the following screen on the execution of the preceding command:

```
(my_env) nathan@nathan-ThinkPad-Twist:~$ conda list
# packages in environment at /home/nathan/anaconda3/envs/my_env:
#
# Name                    Version                   Build  Channel
blas                      1.0                          mkl
ca-certificates           2018.03.07                     0
certifi                   2018.10.15               py37_0
intel-openmp              2019.0                       118
libedit                   3.1.20170329            h6b74fdf_2
libffi                    3.2.1                   hd88cf55_4
libgcc-ng                 8.2.0                   hdf63c60_1
libgfortran-ng            7.3.0                   hdf63c60_0
libstdcxx-ng              8.2.0                   hdf63c60_1
mkl                       2019.0                       118
mkl_fft                   1.0.6              py37h7dd41cf_0
mkl_random                1.0.1              py37h4414c95_1
ncurses                   6.1                     hf484d3e_0
numpy                     1.15.4             py37h1d66e8a_0
numpy-base                1.15.4             py37h81de0dd_0
openssl                   1.1.1                   h7b6447c_0
pip                       18.1                     py37_0
python                    3.7.1                   h0371630_3
readline                  7.0                     h7b6447c_5
setuptools                40.5.0                   py37_0
sqlite                    3.25.2                  h7b6447c_0
tk                        8.6.8                   hbc83047_0
wheel                     0.32.2                   py37_0
xz                        5.2.4                   h14c3975_4
zlib                      1.2.11                  ha838bed_2
```

Recommended libraries

If you choose to manage a smaller environment than the full bundle from Anaconda, I recommend the following essential libraries for data mining. They will be used throughout this book:

- numpy: The fundamental math library for Python. Brings with it the numpy array data structure.
- scipy: Provides science and engineering routines built on the base of the numpy array. This library also has some good statistical functions.
- pandas: Offers relational data tables for storing, labeling, viewing, and manipulating data. You will never look at an array of numbers in the same way for the rest of your career after you've gotten comfortable with pandas and its popular data structure, called a dataframe.

- `matplotlib`: Python's core visualization library with line and scatter plots, bar and pie charts, histograms and spectrograms, and so on.
- `seaborn`: As statistical visualization library. Built on top of `matplotlib` and much easier to use. You can build complicated visual representations with, in many cases, a single line of code. This library takes `pandas dataframes` as input.
- `statsmodels`: Library focused on statistics functions and statistical testing. For example, it has a `.summary()` function that returns helpful summary stats and information about a model you've applied.
- `scikit-learn`: Python's workhorse machine learning library. It is easy to use and is maintained by an army of developers. The best part is the documentation on `http:\\scikit-learn.org`. It is so extensive that one could learn the field of machine learning just by reading though the entirety of it.

 Editorial: Python has become ubiquitous in the fields of advanced data analysis in the last decade. This is partially due to the scripting nature of the language and approachability to non-programmers, but that is not the whole story. The pandas, `scikit-learn`, and `seaborn` libraries are essential to Python's growth in this domain. The power, ease-of-use, well-defined targeted scope, and open source nature of these three libraries are unmatched among free or paid packages. I recommend you learn them inside and out as you embark on a career in data mining.

Summary

This chapter introduced the contents of the book and covered getting started with your software environment. It also covered how to get high-speed Python and popular libraries such as `pandas`, `scikit-learn`, and `seaborn`. After reading this chapter and setting your environment, you should be ready to follow along with the demonstrations throughout the rest of the book.

Basic Terminology and Our End-to-End Example

2

The philosophy behind a quick-start guide is that the topic at hand is best learned by doing. In this chapter, I will present a quick overview of important vocabulary, concepts, and terminology that you need to get started, and then jump directly into a full end-to-end working example of data mining in Python. Later chapters will flesh out the steps in the working example in more detail.

The following topics will be covered in this chapter:

- Basic data terminology
- Basic statistics
- An end-to-end example of data mining in Python

Basic data terminology

This section is meant to be a quick overview of the terms that you should know before you get started. This list is very streamlined and is not exhaustive. Please refer to the suggested reading in `Chapter 1`, *Data Mining and Getting Started with Python Tools*, for wider coverage of domain-specific terminology.

Sample spaces

The sample space is the space that is covered by all the possible outcomes of a measurement. For example, if a feature column in a dataset is populated with the number of days last month that a responder watched television, then the sample space will include all the integers in the $\{0, 1, 2 \ldots 31\}$ set. If a manufacturing tool measures the temperature difference before and after processing a widget, then the sample space is a continuous range from $\{|0-\text{maxT}|\}$, where maxT is the highest temperature that the tool can measure. Data outside the sample space can be a sign of misreporting or a systematic misunderstanding of the problem statement, and should trigger further investigation.

The concept of sample space seems trivial but it's vital for good data mining practice. Not only does it help you to identify outliers or missing and wrong data points, it also helps to orient your mind to the task at hand and understand what the data is meant to represent. Ask yourself this question before you get started: *"What is my sample space?"*

Variable types

Put simply, dependent variables respond to the influence of the independent variables. In data mining, the dependent variables are often called output vars because they are the outcome of whatever underlying mathematical or statistical behavior you are trying to model. Indeed, predictive analytics attempts to model the dependent variables' response to the independent variables in the dataset and, by doing so, predict its output in future events. Practitioners will often refer to independent variables collectively as **X** and dependent variables as **Y**:

- **Independent variables**: The features of a dataset; these are often denoted as **X** in **XY** data terminology.
- **Dependent variables**: The output in response to independent feature variables; the **Y** in **XY** data terminology:

Person	X				Y
	Age	Height	Weight	Training Hours/week	Long Jump
Thomas	12	57.5	73.4	6.5	19.2
Jane	13	65.5	85.3	8.9	25.1
Vaughn	17	71.9	125.9	1.1	14.3
Vera	14	65.3	100.5	7.9	18.3
Vincent	18	70.1	110.7	10.5	21.1
Lei-Ann	12	52.3	70.4	0.5	10.6

 It is important to note that multi-output data is common, so **Y** can be a multi-column matrix as well.

Data types

There are a few different types of data – each reflecting the type of information that is stored. Understanding the differences is vital to dealing with the downstream effects of working with each type. The different data types are introduced as follows:

- `Categorical: Nominal`: Qualitative and with no ordering to the labels. For example, hair color (black, brown, blonde, and red).
- `Categorical: Ordinal`: Qualitative and ordered in some way. For example, satisfaction levels (not, somewhat, neutral, and very).
- `Numerical: Discrete`: Quantitative and with a finite sample space and/or countable infinite discretizations. For example, 1, 2, and 3.
- `Numerical: Continuous`: Quantitative and covering an interval or span of real numbers. For example, all real numbers that span (3.0 - 5.0).

Basic summary statistics

Practitioners in the field of descriptive analytics use a set of four summary statistics to quickly understand a dataset. With practice, you should be able to strengthen your intuition about each one of these statistical measurements. In fact, it's a great place to start with most problem statements that you will face. The four summary statistics are described as follows:

- **Locations**: The location or center of the data; this can be measured by the **mean** (average), **median**, or **mode**. The median is the point of delineation in 50% of the data, and the mode is the most occurring points, or largest part of the distribution.
- **Spread**: How the data is spread around the center; this can be measured with **standard deviation**, which sums the average distance from the mean of each data point, or **variance**, which is the square of the deviation.
- **Shape**: A description of where the center of distribution sits in relation to the mean. This is usually expressed as the **skew** direction. You can refer to the following diagram for a negative skew example. In the case of positive skew, the tail is simply pointed in the opposite direction.
- **Correlation**: The measurement of dependency of one variable against another. The most common measure is the **Pearson correlation coefficient**, which is between -1 (a full negative correlation) and +1 (a full positive correlation). A value of 0 signifies no correlation; this is usually denoted with "r".

Take a look at the following diagram for a visualization of the points described in this section:

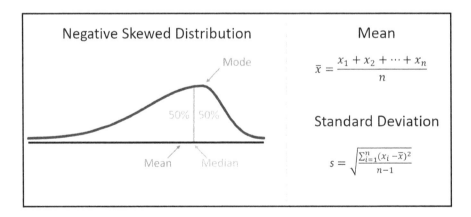

An end-to-end example of data mining in Python

Let's start with a full end-to-end example demonstrating the topics and strategies covered in the rest of the book. Subsequent chapters will go into further detail on each part of the analytical process. I suggest that you read through this example fully before moving on in the book.

Loading data into memory – viewing and managing with ease using pandas

First, we will need to load data into memory so that Python can interact with it. Pandas will be our data management and manipulation library:

```
# load data into Pandas
import pandas as pd
df = pd.read_csv("./data/iris.csv")
```

Let's use some built-in pandas features to do sanity checks on our data load and make sure that we've loaded everything properly. First, we use the `.shape` attribute to check the size of the data printed (as rows and columns). Next, we sanity check the contents of the `DataFrame` with the `.head()` method, which returns the first five lines in a new and smaller `DataFrame` for easy viewing. Finally, we can use the `.describe()` method to show some summary statistics for each feature.

 Pandas has many more sanity check and quick view features. For example, `.tail()` will return the final five lines of the data. Becoming proficient in pandas is undoubtedly worth the time investment. The dedicated chapter that appears later in the book is a good place to start, as well as the essential basic functionality (`https://pandas.pydata.org/pandas-docs/stable/getting_started/basics.html`) page on the pandas documentation site.

```
# sanity check with Pandas
print("shape of data in (rows, columns) is " + str(df.shape))
print(df.head())
print(df.describe().transpose())
```

You will see the following output after executing the preceding code:

```
shape of data in (rows, columns) is (150, 5)
   sepal length in cm  sepal width in cm  petal length in cm  \
0                 5.1                3.5                 1.4
1                 4.9                3.0                 1.4
2                 4.7                3.2                 1.3
3                 4.6                3.1                 1.5
4                 5.0                3.6                 1.4

   petal width in cm species
0                0.2  setosa
1                0.2  setosa
2                0.2  setosa
3                0.2  setosa
4                0.2  setosa
                     count      mean       std  min  25%   50%  75%  max
sepal length in cm   150.0  5.843333  0.828066  4.3  5.1  5.80  6.4  7.9
sepal width in cm    150.0  3.054000  0.433594  2.0  2.8  3.00  3.3  4.4
petal length in cm   150.0  3.758667  1.764420  1.0  1.6  4.35  5.1  6.9
petal width in cm    150.0  1.198667  0.763161  0.1  0.3  1.30  1.8  2.5
```

Plotting and exploring data – harnessing the power of Seaborn

Now let's start our analysis with Seaborn's canned plotting routine called **pairplot** to visualize pairwise feature relationships. You can use this routine to hunt down relationships, candidates for groupings, possible outliers, and an intuition for what downstream strategies to investigate for analysis. Each off-diagonal cell is a pairwise scatter plot and the diagonals are filled with univariate distributions:

```
# explore with Seaborn pairplot
import seaborn as sns
sns.pairplot(df,hue='species')
```

You will see the following output after executing the preceding code:

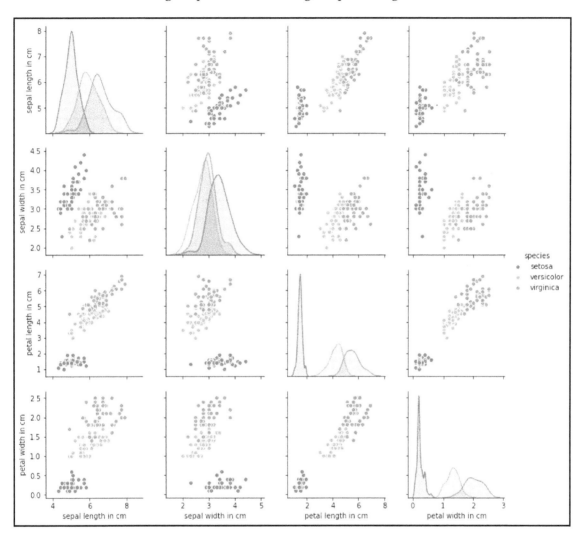

Sometimes, a histogram is easier to use than probability-density plots for understanding a distribution. With Seaborn, we can easily pass the `diag_kind` arg and re-plot it to view the histograms in the diagonals.

Also, we can change the aesthetics with **palette** and **marker** args. You can refer to the Seaborn documentation for more available args; let's do the re-plot as follows:

```
# add histograms to diagonals of Seaborn pairplot
sns.pairplot(df,hue='species',diag_kind='hist',
             palette='bright',markers=['o','x','v'])
```

You will see the following output after executing the preceding code:

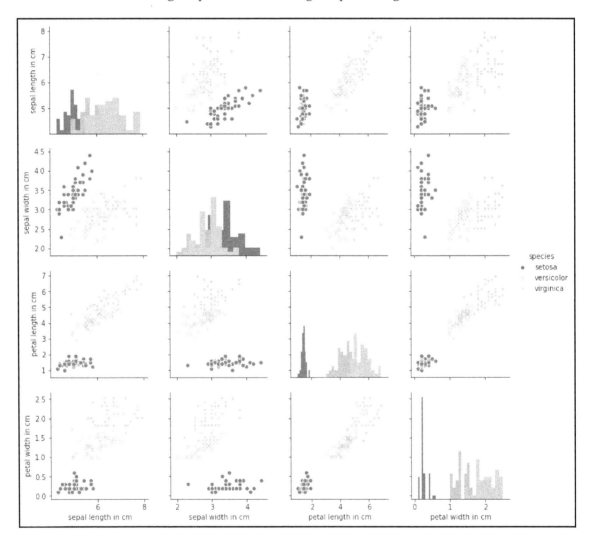

At this point, we can choose two variables and plot them in a scatter plot with Seaborn's `lmplot`. If your dataset has more than five features, important variable relationships may not be shown on the same window of the pair plot. You can use this bivariate scatter plot to isolate and view important pairings:

```
# plot bivariate scatter with Seaborn
sns.lmplot(x='petal length in cm', y='petal width in cm',
           hue="species", data=df, fit_reg=False,
           palette='bright',markers=['o','x','v'])
```

You will see the following output after executing the preceding code:

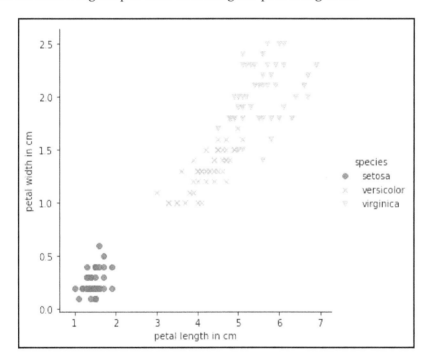

A popular quick-view of a single feature vector is a **violin plot**. Many practitioners prefer violins for understanding raw value distributions and class spreads on a single plot. Each violin is actually the univariate distribution, displayed as probability density, of the values within a given class plotted vertically like a box plot. This concept probably sounds convoluted, but one look at the plot should get the idea across with ease, and that's the idea. The more violin plots you see, the more you will learn to love them:

```
sns.violinplot(x='species',y='petal length in cm', data=df)
```

You will see the following output after executing the preceding code:

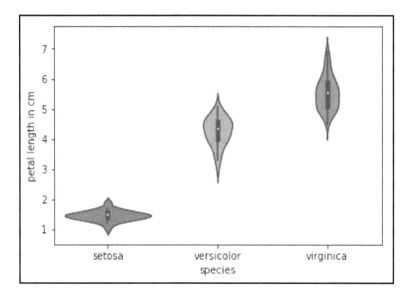

 By default, Seaborn will add the median and interquartile range (middle 50%) to each violin in the plot. You can change this by using the **inner** arg. This is explained in the Seaborn online documentation for violin plots: `https://seaborn.pydata.org/generated/seaborn.violinplot.html`.

Transforming data – PCA and LDA with scikit-learn

Often, a transformation can make data more digestible. In particular, data scientists use transformations to rotate the data about the axis of the most overall or most important variations with the aim of representing similar information with a smaller number of dimensions. We can use the iris dataset as an example to take four features and represent similar information in two dimensions. Let's start with **principal component analysis** (**PCA**) to orient the data onto the axes of the highest variation. The iris set only has four dimensions, but this technique can be used on data with tens or hundreds of features:

```
# reduce dimensions with PCA
from sklearn.decomposition import PCA
pca = PCA(n_components=2)
out_pca = pca.fit_transform(df[['sepal length in cm',
```

```
'sepal width in cm',
'petal length in cm',
'petal width in cm']])
```

Now, let's create a pandas DataFrame with the output data and use the `.head()` sanity check to see what we have:

```
df_pca = pd.DataFrame(data = out_pca, columns = ['pca1', 'pca2'])
print(df_pca.head())
```

You will see the following output after executing the preceding code:

```
        pca1       pca2
0  -2.684207   0.326607
1  -2.715391  -0.169557
2  -2.889820  -0.137346
3  -2.746437  -0.311124
4  -2.728593   0.333925
```

This looks good, but we are missing the target or label column (species). Let's add the column by concatenating with the original DataFrame. This gives us a PCA DataFrame (df_pca) that is ready for downstream work and predictions. Then, let's plot it and see what our transformed data looks like plotted on just two dimensions:

```
df_pca = pd.concat([df_pca, df[['species']]], axis = 1)
print(df_pca.head())
sns.lmplot(x="pca1", y="pca2", hue="species", data=df_pca, fit_reg=False)
```

You will see the following output after executing the preceding code:

```
        pca1       pca2 species
0  -2.684207   0.326607  setosa
1  -2.715391  -0.169557  setosa
2  -2.889820  -0.137346  setosa
3  -2.746437  -0.311124  setosa
4  -2.728593   0.333925  setosa
```

The following plot is obtained after the execution of same code snippet:

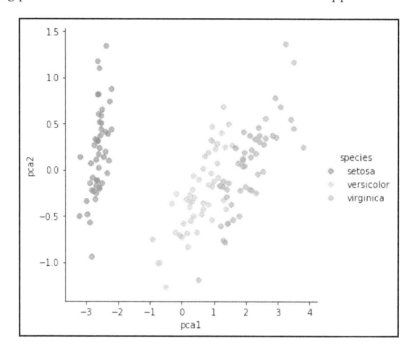

We now have our higher-dimensional data represented in two easily-digestible and plottable dimensions. However, can we do better? The goal of PCA is to orient the data in the direction of the greatest variation. However, it ignores some important information from our dataset – for instance, the labels are not used; perhaps we can extract even better transformation vectors if we include the labels. The most popular labeled dimension-reduction technique is called **linear discriminant analysis** (**LDA**). The following math will group by class labels, and then find the direction of most separation between the classes:

Ignoring labels in the transformation step can be desirable for some problem statements (especially those with unreliable class labels) to avoid pulling the reduced component vectors in an unhelpful direction. For this reason, I recommend that you always start with PCA before deciding whether you need to do any further work or not. Indeed, unless your dataset is large, the computation time for PCA is short, so there's no harm in starting here.

```
# reduce dimensions with LDA
from sklearn.discriminant_analysis import LinearDiscriminantAnalysis
lda = LinearDiscriminantAnalysis(n_components=2)
```

```
# format dataframe
out_lda = lda.fit_transform(X=df.iloc[:,:4], y=df['species'])
df_lda = pd.DataFrame(data = out_lda, columns = ['lda1', 'lda2'])
df_lda = pd.concat([df_lda, df[['species']]], axis = 1)

# sanity check
print(df_lda.head())

# plot
sns.lmplot(x="lda1", y="lda2", hue="species", data=df_lda, fit_reg=False)
```

You will see the following output after executing the preceding code:

```
       lda1      lda2 species
0 -8.084953  0.328454  setosa
1 -7.147163 -0.755473  setosa
2 -7.511378 -0.238078  setosa
3 -6.837676 -0.642885  setosa
4 -8.157814  0.540639  setosa
```

The following plot is obtained after the execution of same code snippet:

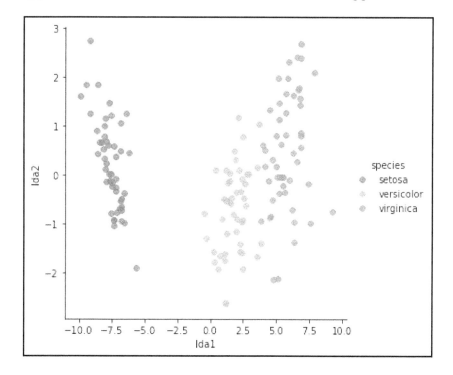

The scatter plots may tempt you into thinking that the PCA and LDA techniques performed the same transformation on the data. Let's look a little closer at the first component of each using the powerful violin plot routine. First, we will begin with PCA, as follows:

```
sns.violinplot(x='species',y='pca1', data=df_pca).set_title("Violin plot:
Feature = PCA_1")
```

You will see the following output after executing the preceding code:

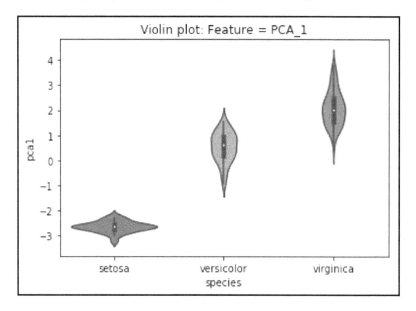

Now, let's plot the first LDA component, as follows:

```
sns.violinplot(x='species',y='lda1', data=df_lda).set_title("Violin plot:
Feature = LDA_1")
```

You will see the following output after executing the preceding code:

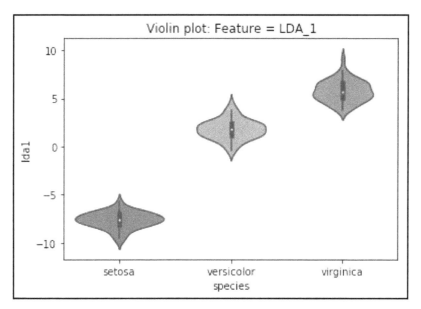

Quantifying separations – k-means clustering and the silhouette score

The most difficult class separation in this dataset is versicolor and virginica. The violins for each of these classes tell us that the two techniques actually produce different results. Using the setosa distribution as a reference in both plots, the LDA versicolor distribution is tighter (that is, wider and shorter) than the PCA one, causing its interquartile range to be further separated from the interquartile range of the virginica distribution. If this analysis is not rigorous enough for you, we can easily quantify this difference by using a clustering algorithm on the data. Let's use the k-means clustering algorithm to mathematically group the data together, and then use the quantitative metric called silhouette coefficient to score the tightness of the resulting clusters – a higher score means tighter clusters. Since the k-means algorithm is very straightforward and the quality of the grouping is directly related to the quality of the input data, tighter clusters will prove that the input features separate the classes better:

```
# cluster With k-means and check silhouette score
from sklearn.cluster import KMeans
from sklearn.metrics import silhouette_score
```

```
# initialize k-means algo object
kmns = KMeans(n_clusters=3, random_state=42)

# fit algo to pca and find silhouette score
out_kms_pca = kmns.fit_predict(out_pca)
silhouette = silhouette_score(out_pca, out_kms_pca)
print("PCA silhouette score = " + str(silhouette))

# fit algo to lda and find silhouette score
out_kms_lda = kmns.fit_predict(out_lda)
silhouette = silhouette_score(out_lda, out_kms_lda)
print("LDA silhouette score = %2f " % silhouette)
```

The following output shows that the LDA classes are better separated:

```
PCA silhouette score = 0.598
LDA silhouette score = 0.656
```

This makes sense because the LDA function had more information, namely, the classes to be separated.

Making decisions or predictions

Before we build a prediction, we need to separate our data into training and test sets. Model validation is a large and very important topic that will be covered later in the book, but for the purpose of this end-to-end example, we will do a basic train-test split. We will then build the prediction model on the training data and score it on the test data using the F_1 score.

I recommend using a random seed for the most randomized data selection. This seed tells the pseudo-random number generator where to begin its randomization routine. The result is the same random choice every time. In this example, I've used the random seed when splitting into test and training sets. Now, if I stop working on the project and pick it back up later, I can split with the random seed and get the exact same training and test sets. I used 42 for my seed as it is common in the field due to the popularity of *The Hitchhiker's Guide to the Galaxy* by Douglas Adams.

```
# Split into train/validation/test set
from sklearn.model_selection import train_test_split
df_train, df_test = train_test_split(df_lda, test_size=0.3,
random_state=42)
```

```
# Sanity check
print('train set shape = ' + str(df_train.shape))
print('test set shape = ' + str(df_test.shape))
print(df_train.head())
```

You will see the following output after executing the preceding code:

```
train set shape = (105, 3)
test set shape = (45, 3)
         lda1      lda2    species
81   0.598443 -1.923348  versicolor
133  3.809721 -0.934519   virginica
137  4.993563  0.184883   virginica
75   1.439522 -0.123147  versicolor
109  6.872871  2.694581   virginica
```

Now we can move on to predictions. Let's first try a **Support Vector Machine** (**SVM**) by using the **Support Vector Classifier** (**SVC**) module. Notice how the classifier objects in scikit-learn have similar API calls to the PCA and LDA transforms from earlier. So, once you gain an understanding of the library, you can learn how to apply different transformations, classifiers, or other methods with very little effort:

```
# classify with SVM
from sklearn.svm import SVC
from sklearn.metrics import f1_score
clf = SVC(kernel='rbf', C=0.8, gamma=10)
clf.fit(df_train[['lda1', 'lda2']], df_train['species'])

# predict on test set
y_pred = clf.predict(df_test[['lda1', 'lda2']])
f1 = f1_score(df_test['species'], y_pred, average='weighted')

# check prediction score
print("f1 score for SVM classifier = %2f " % f1)
```

The F_1 score for this classifier is 0.79, as calculated on the test set. At this point, we can try to change a model setting and fit it again. The C parameter was set to 0.8 in our first run – using the C=0.8 arg in the instantiation of the clf object. C is a penalty term and is called a **hyperparameter**; this means that it is a setting that an analyst can use to steer a fit in a certain direction. Here, we will use the penalty C hyperparameter to tune the model towards better predictions. Let's change it from 0.8 to 1, which will effectively raise the penalty term.

C is the penalty term in an SVM. It controls how large the penalty is for a mis-classed example internally during the model fit. For a utilitarian understanding, it is called the soft margin penalty because it tunes how hard or soft the resulting separation line is drawn. Common hyperparameters for SVMs will be covered in more detail in a later chapter.

```
# classify with SVM
from sklearn.svm import SVC
from sklearn.metrics import f1_score
clf = SVC(kernel='rbf', C=1, gamma=10)
clf.fit(df_train[['lda1', 'lda2']], df_train['species'])
y_pred = clf.predict(df_test[['lda1', 'lda2']])
f1 = f1_score(df_test['species'], y_pred, average='weighted')
print("f1 score for SVM classifier = %2f " % f1)
```

The F_1 score for this classifier is now 0.85. The obvious next step is to tune the parameters and maximize the F_1 score. Of course, it will be very tedious to change a parameter (refit, analyze, and repeat). Instead, you can employ a **grid search** to automate this parameterization. Grid search and **cross-validation** will be covered in more detail in later chapters. An alternative method to employing a grid search is to choose an algorithm that doesn't require tuning. A popular algorithm that requires little-to-no tuning is **Random Forest**. The forest refers to how the method adds together multiple decision trees into a voted prediction:

```
# classify with RF
from sklearn.ensemble import RandomForestClassifier
clf = RandomForestClassifier(n_estimators=2, random_state=42)
clf.fit(df_train[['lda1', 'lda2']], df_train['species'])
y_pred = clf.predict(df_test[['lda1', 'lda2']])
f1 = f1_score(df_test['species'], y_pred, average='weighted')

# check prediction score
print("f1 score for SVM classifier = %2f " % f1)
```

The F_1 score for this classifier is 0.96, that is, with no tuning. The Random Forest method will be discussed in more detail in later chapters.

Summary

This chapter covered the basic statistics and data terminology that are required for working in data mining. The final portion of the chapter was dedicated to a full working example, which combined the types of techniques that will be introduced later on in this book. After reading this chapter, you should have a better understanding of the thought processes behind analysis and the common steps taken to address a problem statement that you may encounter in the field. The subsequent chapters will explore each aspect of the example in more depth, with the next chapter focusing on collecting data, loading it into memory, and exploring it with ease.

3
Collecting, Exploring, and Visualizing Data

As a first step, it is important to understand how to acquire data and how to access it in computer memory. Once data is loaded, sound practices for exploration can save time downstream. This chapter will start by showing you how to interact with different data sources such as databases, disks, and streaming. Despite the practicality of these topics, many new analysts overlook them. Indeed, you cannot actually do any work if you cannot get past this beginning step. The second half of the chapter will introduce you to Seaborn for visualizing data, and then recommend types of plots for relevant and popular problem statements.

The following topics will be covered in this chapter:

- Types of data sources and loading into pandas
- Access, search, and sanity checks with pandas
- Basic plotting in Seaborn
- Relevant types of plots for visualizing data

Types of data sources and loading into pandas

This part of the chapter will show you how to load data in the computer memory. This is, of course, essential to all the downstream work and analysis that you plan to do.

Databases

A relational database is one of the most common ways that enterprises can store data. So, loading from and interacting with databases is essential for most fieldwork. The Python library that we will use is sqlite3 and is included in Anaconda's package. Let's begin by connecting to the database, which is stored in a .db file, and included with the book materials. After we connect to the database, we will create a cursor object that we will use to traverse the object during a query. Next, we will select the entire contents of the boston table with the * condition and limit the rows to five (only so that we can display the output without overloading our console). Finally, we will execute() the query and fetchall(). The data returned from the query is controlled by the search teams (select and limit, in this case). The next section will introduce more common terms used for queries:

```python
import sqlite3
sqlite_file = './data/boston.db'

# connecting to the database file
conn = sqlite3.connect(sqlite_file)

# initialize a cursor obect
cur = conn.cursor()

# define a traversing search
cur.execute("select * from boston limit 5;")

# fetch and print
data = cur.fetchall()
print(data)
```

The output from the print() statement is 5 records, each with 15 entries, which correspond to the rows and columns of the data table, respectively:

```
[(0, 0.00632, 18.0, 2.31, 0.0, 0.538, 6.575, 65.2, 4.09, 1.0, 296.0, 15.3, 396.9, 4.98, 24.0), (1, 0.02731, 0.0, 7.07, 0.0, 0.4
69, 6.421, 78.9, 4.9671, 2.0, 242.0, 17.8, 396.9, 9.14, 21.6), (2, 0.02729, 0.0, 7.07, 0.0, 0.469, 7.185, 61.1, 4.9671, 2.0, 24
2.0, 17.8, 392.83, 4.03, 34.7), (3, 0.03237, 0.0, 2.18, 0.0, 0.458, 6.998, 45.8, 6.0622, 3.0, 222.0, 18.7, 394.63, 2.94, 33.4),
(4, 0.06905, 0.0, 2.18, 0.0, 0.458, 7.147, 54.2, 6.0622, 3.0, 222.0, 18.7, 396.9, 5.33, 36.2)]
```

 For our example, we use the included database (.db) file in the place of an actual remote database. This means that we will connect to this file. In practice, you will connect to a remote location by using a network address and login credentials.

Basic Structured Query Language (SQL) queries

SQL is the language that is used to interact with data in a database. There are different variants of query syntax among versions, but the general idea is the same across all of them. The concept of SQL-searching is best conveyed by examples, so this section will demonstrate some common SQL search terms with easily adaptable and transferable examples.

 These examples build on the connection and cursor objects from the last section.

Only select from the `ZN` column, and filter in only the preceding values:

```
cur.execute("select ZN from boston where ZN > 0.0;")
data = cur.fetchall()
print(data)
```

The output from the `print()` statement is hard to understand because there is no language or structure:

```
[(18.0,), (12.5,), (12.5,), (12.5,), (12.5,), (12.5,), (12.5,), (12.5,), (75.0,), (75.0,), (21.0,), (21.0,), (21.0,), (21.0,),
(75.0,), (90.0,), (85.0,), (100.0,), (25.0,), (25.0,), (25.0,), (25.0,), (25.0,), (25.0,), (17.5,), (80.0,), (80.0,), (12.5,),
(12.5,), (12.5,), (25.0,), (25.0,), (25.0,), (25.0,), (28.0,), (28.0,), (28.0,), (45.0,), (45.0,), (45.0,), (45.0,), (45.0,),
(45.0,), (60.0,), (60.0,), (80.0,), (80.0,), (80.0,), (80.0,), (95.0,), (95.0,), (82.5,), (82.5,), (95.0,), (95.0,), (30.0,),
(30.0,), (30.0,), (30.0,), (30.0,), (30.0,), (22.0,), (22.0,), (22.0,), (22.0,), (22.0,), (22.0,), (22.0,), (22.0,), (22.0,),
(22.0,), (80.0,), (80.0,), (90.0,), (20.0,), (20.0,), (20.0,), (20.0,), (20.0,), (20.0,), (20.0,), (20.0,), (20.0,), (20.0,),
(20.0,), (20.0,), (20.0,), (20.0,), (20.0,), (20.0,), (20.0,), (40.0,), (40.0,), (40.0,), (40.0,), (40.0,), (20.0,), (20.0,),
(20.0,), (20.0,), (90.0,), (90.0,), (55.0,), (80.0,), (52.5,), (52.5,), (52.5,), (80.0,), (80.0,), (80.0,), (70.0,), (70.0,),
(70.0,), (34.0,), (34.0,), (34.0,), (33.0,), (33.0,), (33.0,), (33.0,), (35.0,), (35.0,), (35.0,), (55.0,), (55.0,), (85.0,),
(80.0,), (40.0,), (40.0,), (60.0,), (60.0,), (90.0,), (80.0,), (80.0,)]
```

There are two methods that you can use to deal with this unstructured program. First, you can code around it and do the bookkeeping yourself with mapping that labels this output with the `ZN` column and any other constraints in the search. Alternatively, you can use pandas' built-in SQL capability and put the results of the queries directly into a DataFrame. I recommend the latter strategy, and will demonstrate its power in the rest of the section.

First, let's duplicate our original query for the entire table, which was limited to 5 rows. Please note that the actual search syntax (`select * from boston limit 5`) is the same as the direct sqlite3 code that we passed earlier, so there's not much new to learn:

```
import pandas as pd
# get all data inside boston table limited to 5 rows
df = pd.read_sql_query("select * from boston limit 5;", conn)
print("df.shape = " + str(df.shape))
```

You will see the following output after executing the preceding code:

```
df.shape = (5, 15)
```

We limited our original query example to 5 lines so that we wouldn't overwhelm our console. Since we are now working with pandas, this is no longer needed. Additionally, we now have all of the powerful pandas data analysis functions at our disposal. Now, let's grab the whole table and use pandas to sanity check with the `head()` method and print our summary for us with the `describe()` method:

```
# get all data inside boston table
df = pd.read_sql_query("select * from boston;", conn)
print("df.shape = " + str(df.shape))
print("Sanity check with Pandas head():")
print(df.head())
print("Summarize with Pandas describe():")
print(df.describe().transpose())
```

You will see the following output after executing the preceding code:

```
df.shape = (506, 15)
Sanity check with Pandas head():
   record    CRIM    ZN  INDUS  CHAS    NOX     RM   AGE     DIS  RAD    TAX  LSTAT  MEDV
0       0  0.00632  18.0   2.31   0.0  0.538  6.575  65.2  4.0900  1.0  296.0   4.98  24.0
1       1  0.02731   0.0   7.07   0.0  0.469  6.421  78.9  4.9671  2.0  242.0   9.14  21.6
2       2  0.02729   0.0   7.07   0.0  0.469  7.185  61.1  4.9671  2.0  242.0   4.03  34.7
3       3  0.03237   0.0   2.18   0.0  0.458  6.998  45.8  6.0622  3.0  222.0   2.94  33.4
4       4  0.06905   0.0   2.18   0.0  0.458  7.147  54.2  6.0622  3.0  222.0   5.33  36.2

Summarize with Pandas describe():
        count        mean         std        min         25%        50%         75%        max
record  506.0  252.500000  146.213884    0.00000  126.250000  252.50000  378.750000  505.0000
CRIM    506.0    3.593761    8.596783    0.00632    0.082045    0.25651    3.647423   88.9762
ZN      506.0   11.363636   23.322453    0.00000    0.000000    0.00000   12.500000  100.0000
INDUS   506.0   11.136779    6.860353    0.46000    5.190000    9.69000   18.100000   27.7400
CHAS    506.0    0.069170    0.253994    0.00000    0.000000    0.00000    0.000000    1.0000
NOX     506.0    0.554695    0.115878    0.38500    0.449000    0.53800    0.624000    0.8710
RM      506.0    6.284634    0.702617    3.56100    5.885500    6.20850    6.623500    8.7800
AGE     506.0   68.574901   28.148861    2.90000   45.025000   77.50000   94.075000  100.0000
DIS     506.0    3.795043    2.105710    1.12960    2.100175    3.20745    5.188425   12.1265
RAD     506.0    9.549407    8.707259    1.00000    4.000000    5.00000   24.000000   24.0000
TAX     506.0  408.237154  168.537116  187.00000  279.000000  330.00000  666.000000  711.0000
LSTAT   506.0   12.653063    7.141062    1.73000    6.950000   11.36000   16.955000   37.9700
MEDV    506.0   22.532806    9.197104    5.00000   17.025000   21.20000   25.000000   50.0000
```

Viewing these few lines of code should ignite your imagination. Hopefully, the power of pandas and Python's interactive console becomes immediately apparent and you can see why Python has been adopted as the default data mining and analytics language by the majority of new users in the last decade. Seaborn (plotting) and Scikit-learn (machine learning) are just as powerful and complete as the Python data mining package. You can learn these packages and wield them for power in analysis.

Let's continue with a few more helpful examples, as follows:

```
# get all data inside boston table that has ZN values greater 0
df = pd.read_sql_query("select * from boston where ZN > 0.0;", conn)
print("df.shape = " + str(df.shape))
```

You will see the following output after executing the preceding code:

```
df.shape = (134, 15)
```

Now, let's chain a couple of `sql` commands together, and then filter in the records that are greater than `250`:

```
# same as above with additional filtering in of records greater than 250
df = pd.read_sql_query("select * from boston where ZN > 0.0 and record >
250;", conn)
print("df.shape = " + str(df.shape))
```

You will see the following output after executing the preceding code:

```
df.shape = (66, 15)
```

For long queries, it is conventional to spread the code over multiple short lines for easy reading; consider the following example:

```
# example of multiline search syntax
df = pd.read_sql_query("""
                        select record, ZN, AGE, TAX from boston
                        where ZN > 0.0 and CRIM < 2.5;
                        """,
                        conn)
```

Note that if you make changes to the DataFrame and then want to commit these back to the SQL database, you can use the built-in pandas function for committing:

```
# use Pandas 'to_sql' method to commit changes to connection
df.to_sql("./data/boston_updated", conn, if_exists="replace")
# close connection
conn.close()
```

Disks

Often, data is already stored locally on a disk, such as on a hard drive or on portable media. Loading data into pandas from a disk is simple if the file is in .csv format:

```
# load from file
df = pd.read_csv("./data/iris.csv")
```

Saving the DataFrame changes to a file is also simple, as shown in the following code:

```
# make some changes
# create an index
df.index.name = "record"
df['species'] = "new-species"
print(df.head())

# save to file
df.to_csv("./data/iris_updated.csv", index=True)
```

Pandas also has built-in loading routines for files in the HTML, JSON, or Excel format. The pandas I/O guide is a good place to look up the syntax for your specific file. You can refer to the guide at https://pandas.pydata.org/pandas-docs/stable/reference/io.html.

Web sources

Many datasets are made available on the web. If you have the address, then you can pull them from inside your Python script. Additionally, Scikit-learn and Seaborn have some built-in datasets that you can use. Depending on the distribution that you acquire, the datasets may or may not come bundled. If they are not bundled, then the first time that you try to load them, Python will look online and download the dataset for you, and then store a local copy for later use.

From URLs

To pull the dataset from the URL, you can use the following code:

```
# load from web URL
url =
"https://archive.ics.uci.edu/ml/machine-learning-databases/iris/iris.data"
names = ['sepal length in cm', 'sepal width in cm', 'petal length in cm',
        'petal width in cm', 'species']
df = pd.read_csv(url, names=names)
```

From Scikit-learn and Seaborn-included sets

Some datasets come built-in with Scikit-learn and Seaborn. These are often used for testing and demonstration purposes.

The following is a Scikit-learn example (see `https://scikit-learn.org/stable/datasets/index.html`):

```
# load from web Scikit-learn
from sklearn.datasets import load_iris
dataset = load_iris()
df = pd.DataFrame(dataset.data, columns=dataset.feature_names)
df['species'] = dataset.target
```

The following is a Seaborn example (see `https://seaborn.pydata.org/generated/seaborn.load_dataset.html`):

```
# load from Seaborn
import seaborn as sns
df = sns.load_dataset("flights")
```

Access, search, and sanity checks with pandas

Pandas includes some built-in access functions and search/filter functions to make life easier for users. Pandas also has some sanity checks that are available for you to quickly view your data and ensure that you have the correct batch loaded. For example, we've used the `head()` method, which displays the first five rows with column names, as a way to check which data we loaded in the beginning of this chapter. Don't by shy about sanity checks; if your company has a lot of money riding on the outcome of your analysis, then the last thing you want to do is to mistakenly work with the wrong data loaded.

For ad hoc work in the IPython console, you don't have to include print statements in order to send your output to a console. For example, you can simply pass `df.head()` into the IPython console and return the first five rows. This trick applies to most pandas and Seaborn-bundled methods. This is how many Python users apply trial and error quickly to their problem statements. If, however, you are passing your code through a normal Python interpreter, then you will need to call this method with `print(df.head())` in order to print to the console. I use `print()` statements in this section, but feel free to play around in the IPython notebooks that are included and get a feel for using them without the `print()` statements.

For more helpful methods, check out the official pandas documentation. Just about every practitioner I know bookmarks this page and refers to it constantly: `https://pandas.pydata.org/pandas-docs/stable/user_guide/indexing.html`.

Before we move on, first load the data from the included `boston.db` file, as follows:

```
import pandas as pd
import sqlite3
sqlite_file = './data/boston.db'
# Connecting to the database file
conn = sqlite3.connect(sqlite_file)


df = pd.read_sql_query("select * from boston;", conn)
print("df.shape = " + str(df.shape))
df.set_index("record", inplace=True)
conn.close()
```

Now let's take look at a list of the most common pandas methods that many practitioners use almost daily, with the output shown for all the print statements:

```
# print first 5 rows with column names
print(df.head())
```

You will see the following output after executing the preceding code:

	record	CRIM	ZN	INDUS	CHAS	NOX	RM	AGE	DIS	RAD	TAX	LSTAT	MEDV
0	0	0.00632	18.0	2.31	0.0	0.538	6.575	65.2	4.0900	1.0	296.0	4.98	24.0
1	1	0.02731	0.0	7.07	0.0	0.469	6.421	78.9	4.9671	2.0	242.0	9.14	21.6
2	2	0.02729	0.0	7.07	0.0	0.469	7.185	61.1	4.9671	2.0	242.0	4.03	34.7
3	3	0.03237	0.0	2.18	0.0	0.458	6.998	45.8	6.0622	3.0	222.0	2.94	33.4
4	4	0.06905	0.0	2.18	0.0	0.458	7.147	54.2	6.0622	3.0	222.0	5.33	36.2

Let's use some more pandas sanity checks to understand more about the data that we've loaded:

```
# get amount of rows and columns
print(df.shape)
# get columns in the dataframe
print(df.columns)
```

You will see the following output after executing the preceding code:

```
(506, 14)
 Index(['CRIM', 'ZN', 'INDUS', 'CHAS', 'NOX', 'RM', 'AGE', 'DIS', 'RAD',
'TAX',
   'PTRATIO', 'B', 'LSTAT', 'MEDV'],)
```

Now, use the `.describe()` method to easily get some summary statistics, as follows:

```
# get statistical summary
df.describe()
# view in transposed form
print(df.describe().transpose())
```

You will see the following output after executing the preceding code:

	count	mean	std	min	25%	50%	75%	max
record	506.0	252.500000	146.213884	0.00000	126.250000	252.50000	378.750000	505.0000
CRIM	506.0	3.593761	8.596783	0.00632	0.082045	0.25651	3.647423	88.9762
ZN	506.0	11.363636	23.322453	0.00000	0.000000	0.00000	12.500000	100.0000
INDUS	506.0	11.136779	6.860353	0.46000	5.190000	9.69000	18.100000	27.7400
CHAS	506.0	0.069170	0.253994	0.00000	0.000000	0.00000	0.000000	1.0000
NOX	506.0	0.554695	0.115878	0.38500	0.449000	0.53800	0.624000	0.8710
RM	506.0	6.284634	0.702617	3.56100	5.885500	6.20850	6.623500	8.7800
AGE	506.0	68.574901	28.148861	2.90000	45.025000	77.50000	94.075000	100.0000
DIS	506.0	3.795043	2.105710	1.12960	2.100175	3.20745	5.188425	12.1265
RAD	506.0	9.549407	8.707259	1.00000	4.000000	5.00000	24.000000	24.0000
TAX	506.0	408.237154	168.537116	187.00000	279.000000	330.00000	666.000000	711.0000
LSTAT	506.0	12.653063	7.141062	1.73000	6.950000	11.36000	16.955000	37.9700
MEDV	506.0	22.532806	9.197104	5.00000	17.025000	21.20000	25.000000	50.0000

We can use pandas' built-in `.min()`, `.max()`, `.mean()`, and `.median()` methods as well; let's do that now:

```
# get max and min values
df.max()
df.min()
# get mean and median values
df.mean()
print(df.median())
```

You will see the following output after executing the preceding code (with median values for every column):

```
CRIM         0.25651
ZN           0.00000
INDUS        9.69000
CHAS         0.00000
NOX          0.53800
RM           6.20850
AGE         77.50000
DIS          3.20745
RAD          5.00000
TAX        330.00000
PTRATIO     19.05000
B          391.44000
LSTAT       11.36000
MEDV        21.20000
dtype: float64
```

Now, let's get the index of the maximum and minimum values using the `.idmax()` and `.idmin()` methods:

```
# get index of max and min values
df.idxmax()
print(df.idxmin())
```

You will see the following output after executing the preceding code (with the index/row location of the minimum values in each column):

```
CRIM         0
ZN           1
INDUS      195
CHAS         0
NOX        286
RM         365
AGE         41
DIS        372
RAD          0
TAX        353
PTRATIO    196
B          450
LSTAT      161
MEDV       398
dtype: int64
```

Additionally, we can get specific rows with ease:

```
# get first row of data (index=0)
df.loc[0]
# get third row of data (index=2)
df.loc[2]
# get first row of CRIM column
print(df.loc[0]['CRIM'])
```

You will see the following output after executing the preceding code (index=0 of the CRIM column):

```
 0.00632
```

We can also isolate single columns, as follows:

```
# isolate single columns
df['AGE'].mean()
df['MEDV'].idxmax()
print(df['AGE'].idxmin())
```

You will see the following output after executing the preceding code (with the index of the minimum values of the AGE column):

41

We can even sort according to specific columns with the by arg. Note that the pandas .sort() method uses ascending order by default:

```
# sort (ascending by default)
df.sort_values(by = 'ZN')
# sort descending
df.sort_values(by = 'ZN', ascending = False)
print(df.sort_values(by = 'ZN', ascending = False).head())
```

You will see the following output after executing the preceding code (the full table is sorted in descending order on the ZN column):

record	CRIM	ZN	INDUS	CHAS	NOX	RM	AGE	DIS	RAD	TAX	LSTAT	MEDV
57	0.01432	100.0	1.32	0.0	0.4110	6.816	40.5	8.3248	5.0	256.0	3.95	31.6
204	0.02009	95.0	2.68	0.0	0.4161	8.034	31.9	5.1180	4.0	224.0	2.88	50.0
203	0.03510	95.0	2.68	0.0	0.4161	7.853	33.2	5.1180	4.0	224.0	3.81	48.5
200	0.01778	95.0	1.47	0.0	0.4030	7.135	13.9	7.6534	3.0	402.0	4.45	32.9
199	0.03150	95.0	1.47	0.0	0.4030	6.975	15.3	7.6534	3.0	402.0	4.56	34.9

The previous code snippet only produces a sorted view of the data. It's essentially a disposable, one-time use representation of the data in sorted form. The original data in the memory has not been altered. A permanent sort of a pandas DataFrame requires the `inplace` arg.

Now, let's do a permanent sort on the table with the `inplace` arg, permanently changing how it's stored in memory:

```
# permanently sort the table
df.sort_values(by = 'ZN', inplace=True)
# now call df.head() on permanently sorted table
print(df.head())
```

You will see the following output after executing the preceding code (this is the same as the previous output, as the change is permanent):

	CRIM	ZN	INDUS	CHAS	NOX	RM	AGE	DIS	RAD	TAX	LSTAT	MEDV
record												
57	0.01432	100.0	1.32	0.0	0.4110	6.816	40.5	8.3248	5.0	256.0	3.95	31.6
204	0.02009	95.0	2.68	0.0	0.4161	8.034	31.9	5.1180	4.0	224.0	2.88	50.0
203	0.03510	95.0	2.68	0.0	0.4161	7.853	33.2	5.1180	4.0	224.0	3.81	48.5
200	0.01778	95.0	1.47	0.0	0.4030	7.135	13.9	7.6534	3.0	402.0	4.45	32.9
199	0.03150	95.0	1.47	0.0	0.4030	6.975	15.3	7.6534	3.0	402.0	4.56	34.9

In case we change our minds and want to undo the permanent sort, we can sort according to the original index column and get our original data back:

```
# sort back on index
df.sort_values(by = 'record', inplace=True)
print(df.head())
```

You will see the following output after executing the preceding code (revert back to original table sorted by index):

	record	CRIM	ZN	INDUS	CHAS	NOX	RM	AGE	DIS	RAD	TAX	LSTAT	MEDV
0	0	0.00632	18.0	2.31	0.0	0.538	6.575	65.2	4.0900	1.0	296.0	4.98	24.0
1	1	0.02731	0.0	7.07	0.0	0.469	6.421	78.9	4.9671	2.0	242.0	9.14	21.6
2	2	0.02729	0.0	7.07	0.0	0.469	7.185	61.1	4.9671	2.0	242.0	4.03	34.7
3	3	0.03237	0.0	2.18	0.0	0.458	6.998	45.8	6.0622	3.0	222.0	2.94	33.4
4	4	0.06905	0.0	2.18	0.0	0.458	7.147	54.2	6.0622	3.0	222.0	5.33	36.2

As a final example, let's chain together a couple of filters and use the `.describe()` method for some summary statistics of the smaller, filtered dataset:

```
# filter dataframe to show only even records
df[df.index % 2 == 0]
# filter dataframe to show only record with AGE greater than 95
```

```
df[df['AGE'] > 95]
# get statistical summary of the filtered table
df[df['AGE'] > 95].describe().transpose()
```

Basic plotting in Seaborn

A thoughtfully-built analytical plot can portray a relationship, trend, or historical recap in a single view. However, from working up and scaling the data, to organizing the labels and choosing a color scheme, to saving in the appropriate format, the steps to build the plot can be long and tedious. Tedious actions are the antithesis to the rapid prototyping that most practitioners want when they decide to use Python for their analytics and data mining. The Seaborn library bundles popular plotting routines in a single function call that is compatible with the IPython console and pandas DataFrames for quick and easy plotting. As a bonus, the plots look wonderful with easy-to-adjust aesthetics.

The pseudocode for plotting in Seaborn is as follows:

```
### this is psuedocode. it will not execute ###
import seaborn as sns
sns.plot_type(dataframe)
```

That's it! Similar to the built-in methods for pandas, these Seaborn routines should excite you by the sheer power that they place at your fingertips with a single line of code.

Popular types of plots for visualizing data

This section will introduce some of the most common plotting routines that are used by analysts in the data mining field. These are the plot types that I see projected on screens in conference rooms on a daily basis at my workplace. The routines in Seaborn all follow similar arguments, conventions, and usage, so after reading through the examples in this section, you should easily be able to build any plot that Seaborn has to offer with ease.

I recommend that you take a look at the example gallery on Seaborn's website. It's a good way to find the plot that you're looking for. The front page includes fully-rendered versions of each plot type and it is available at https://seaborn.pydata.org/examples/index.html.

Scatter plots

The **scatter plot** is the most straightforward way to plot two variables against each other and to visualize relationships between two variables. It is also a good place to start learning the basics of Seaborn. Until recently, the pandas `lmplot()` routine was the most common method for plotting scatters. However, in 2018, pandas introduced a `scatterplot()` routine specifically for these plots. You can use either to get the job done and both are included in following examples. Bear in mind that `lmplot` has a few more features, including the `fit_reg` arg, which tells the plot to fit a regression to the data and plot the line.

Let's start by loading the iris dataset, as follows:

```
import matplotlib.pyplot as plt
import seaborn as sns; sns.set()

# load iris
df = pd.read_csv("./data/iris.csv")
```

First, plot a basic scatter plot with Seaborn, as follows:

```
# scatter plot
sns.scatterplot(x='petal length in cm', y='petal width in cm', data=df)
```

You will see the following output after executing the preceding code:

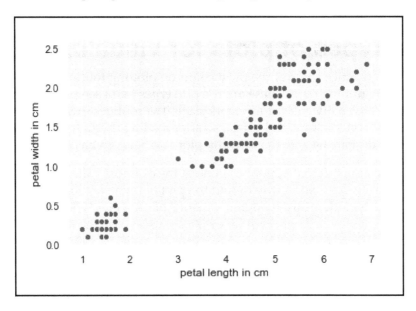

Next, label the data points by color and add the legend with the `hue` argument:

```
sns.scatterplot(x='petal length in cm', y='petal width in cm',
                hue='species', data=df)
```

You will see the following output after executing the preceding code:

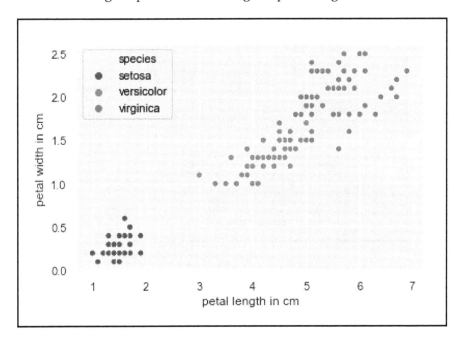

Next, plot scatter points using `lmplot` with `fit_reg=False`:

```
sns.lmplot(x='petal length in cm', y='petal width in cm',
           hue="species", data=df, fit_reg=False,
           palette='bright',markers=['o','x','v'])
```

You will see the following output after executing the preceding code:

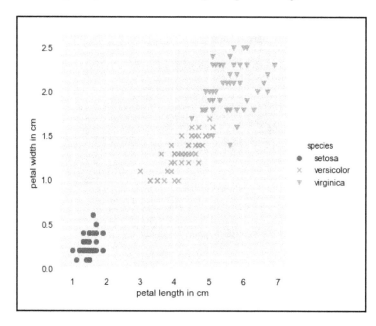

Histograms

A histogram is a bucketed representation of a frequency distribution. Distributions were introduced in Chapter 2, *Basic Terminology and Our End-to-End Example*. Histograms look similar to bar charts, but they are unique in that they only display a single variable with the *y* axis representing the frequency. Let's take a look at an example on the iris dataset:

```
# histogram
sns.distplot(df['petal length in cm'])
```

You will see the following output after executing the preceding code:

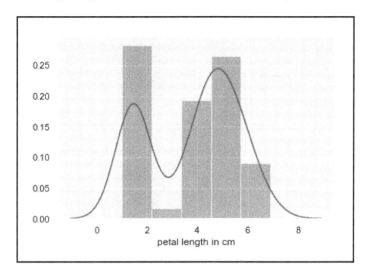

Now, let's specify a larger number of buckets or bins and try to represent the distribution shape more fully:

```
# histogram with 15 bins
sns.distplot(df['petal length in cm'], bins=15)
```

You will see the following output after executing the preceding code:

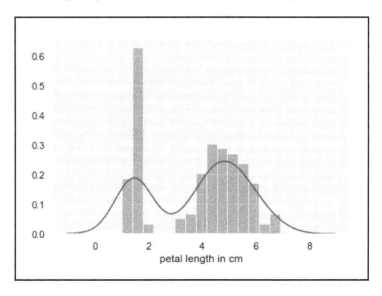

Jointplots

Seaborn has a routine that combines a scatter plot and histogram for two variables. Let's take a look at an example on the iris dataset:

```
# jointplot
sns.jointplot(x='petal length in cm', y='petal width in cm',
              data=df, kind='scatter', marginal_kws=dict(bins=10))
```

You will see the following output after executing the preceding code:

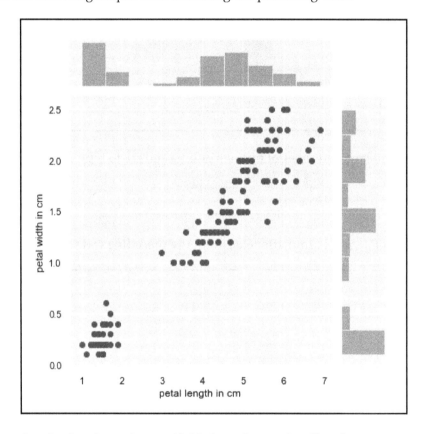

You can also plot the density estimates if this is easier to visualize than scatter points:

```
# jointplot with kde
sns.jointplot(x='petal length in cm', y='petal width in cm',
              data=df, kind='kde')
```

You will see the following output after executing the preceding code:

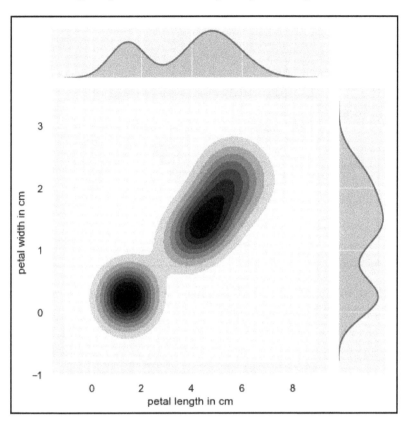

Violin plots

One of the most effective plots for displaying distributions of a single variable broken down by class is a violin plot. These plots are named after their very obvious resemblance to violins.

Let's take a look at an example on the sepal width of the iris dataset:

```
# violin plot
sns.violinplot(x='species',y='sepal width in cm', data=df)
```

You will see the following output after executing the preceding code:

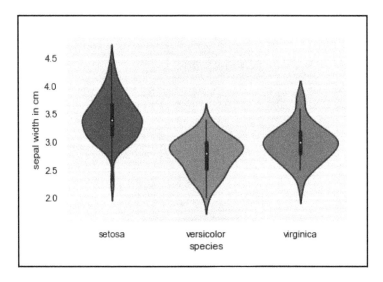

The strength of these violin plots can be visualized when we plot the same violins for a different variable; for example, let's choose `'pedal width in cm'`:

```
# violin plot
sns.violinplot(x='species',y='petal width in cm', data=df)
```

You will see the following output after executing the preceding code:

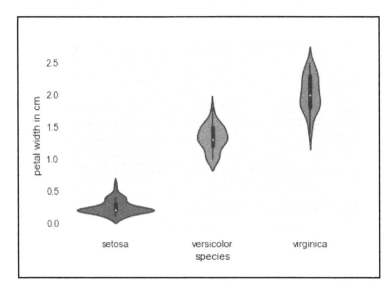

It's obvious to see that the "pedal width" violins are separated far better than the "sepal width" violins. Since each violin represents a class, this means that the "pedal width" variable is better for separating classes from one another.

Pairplots

Seaborn's **pairplot** is a routine in the most literal sense. It will plot scatter plots of multiple variables against each other with histograms plotted in the diagonals. This is a good way to explore a new dataset when you don't know much about the relationships. It is the first place to start when entering the exploratory data analysis stage, especially if you are new to the problem statement.

The pairplot is simple to build, as demonstrated in the following code:

```
# pairplot with all features
sns.pairplot(data=df)
```

However, this will overwhelm your console if the number of features is too large. We can use pandas' list-based column access to lower the number of variables in the pairplot and create a helpful plot. Let's load up the boston dataset and build a pairplot with five selected variables:

```
# pairplot with selected features
vars_to_plot = ['CRIM', 'AGE', 'DIS', 'LSTAT', 'MEDV']
sns.pairplot(data=df, vars=vars_to_plot)
```

You will see the following output after executing the preceding code:

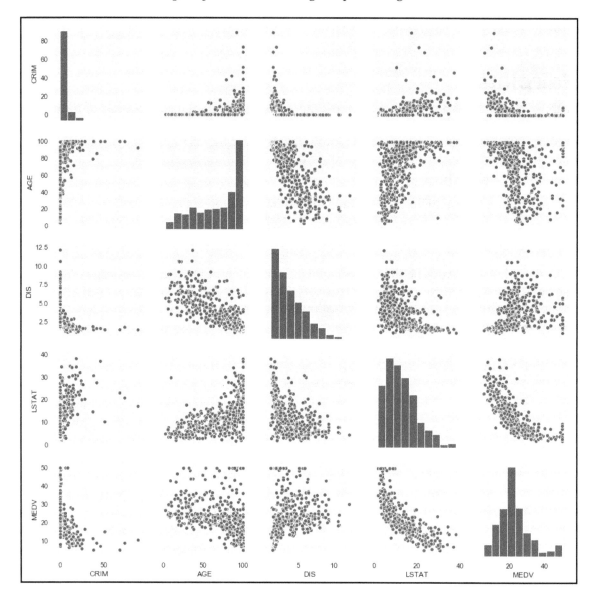

Summary

This chapter covered the basics of loading data from database, disk, and web sources. It also covered basic SQL queries and pandas' access and search functions. The last sections of the chapter introduced common types of plots using Seaborn. You should be able to transfer these basic code examples to many of your analysis projects for data mining. The examples were chosen to demonstrate how to use these libraries, so if your specific need or requirement is not covered, you should be able to replace the method calls with ease, simply by looking up the syntax on the library's website. The next chapter will cover data wrangling and cleaning up data in order to prepare it for analysis.

Cleaning and Readying Data for Analysis

4

Proper preprocessing is important because it conditions data for downstream work and allows users to trust their downstream results. This step is where many practitioners spend the majority of their time, so you should also get comfortable with spending your time on the methods that are discussed here. This chapter will start with cleaning and filtering data input, and then move onto feature selection and dimensional reduction. Feature selection involves searching for relationships and quantifying data/variable quality. So, for all intents and purposes, the mining begins here.

The following topics will be covered in this chapter:

- Cleaning input data
- Working with missing values
- Normalization and standardization
- Handling categorical data
- High-dimensional data and the curse of dimensionality
- Feature selection with filter and wrapper methods
- Feature reduction with transformation

The scikit-learn transformer API

One of the reasons that **scikit-learn** is so popular is due to its ease of use. There are only a few, well thought-out API designs in the scikit-learn library and they are applied in a sweeping manner across many different methods and routines. This chapter will make use of the **transformer API**. It's extremely straightforward and once you understand how to use it, you can try our new transformer methods with ease because they all work the same (that is, they all make use of the transformer API).

The steps for transforming data are given as follows:

1. Import the module.
2. Instantiate the transformer object (**model** in the following diagram).
3. Fit the model to input the training data (**X_train** in the following diagram).
4. Transform the new test data (**X_test** in the following diagram).

These steps can also be represented as a **workflow diagram**, as follows:

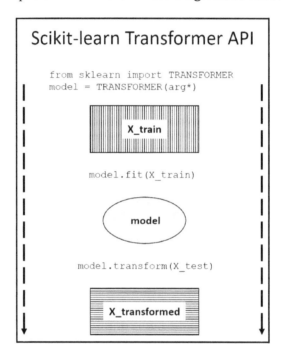

The `fit()` and `transform()` steps can be combined with the `fit_transform()` method, which returns a transformed version of the input data after training. This chapter will use this shortcut method throughout for the sake of clarity and for keeping the code examples short.

 The **estimator API** will be introduced in Chapter 6, *Predictions with Regression and Classification,* and the **pipeline API** will be introduced in Chapter 7, *Building a Data Processing Pipeline and Deploying.*

Cleaning input data

Real data is dirty and its integrity must be ensured before useful insights can be harvested. Missing or corrupt values can contribute to spurious conclusions or completely uncovered insights. In addition to data integrity, feature scaling, and variable types (that is, continuous or discrete) contribute heavily to the effectiveness of downstream methods. I will explain the reasons for these contributions in the dedicated sections for each topic.

Missing values

Missing values can ruin a data mining job. Sometimes, an entire record or row is empty, and at other times a single cell or value inside a record is missing. The latter situation is much harder to spot and, indeed, these missing cells can be quiet killers that cause your analysis job to fail silently for no apparent reason.

In the materials for this book, I've included a version of the iris dataset that purposefully has a few data points and rows removed. Here is an Excel screenshot to illustrate the missing values:

	sepal length	sepal width	petal length	petal width	species
1					
2		3.5	1.4	0.2	setosa
3	4.9	3	1.4	0.2	setosa
4		3.2	1.3	0.2	setosa
5	4.6	3.1	1.5	0.2	setosa
6	5	3.6	1.4	0.2	setosa
7		3.9	1.7	0.4	setosa
8	4.6	3.4	1.4	0.3	setosa
9	5	3.4	1.5	0.2	setosa
10	4.4	2.9	1.4	0.2	setosa
11					
12	5.4	3.7	1.5	0.2	setosa
13	4.8	3.4	1.6	0.2	setosa
14	4.8	3	1.4	0.1	setosa
15	4.3	3	1.1	0.1	setosa
16	5.8	4	1.2	0.2	setosa
17					
18	5.4	3.9	1.3	0.4	setosa

Let's start this section by loading the `iris_missing_values` dataset into memory:

```
# load iris dataset with missing values
import pandas as pd
df = pd.read_csv("./data/iris_missing_values.csv")
df.index.name = "record"
print(df.head())
```

At load time, pandas fills the missing values into a DataFrame with the `NaN` null character:

```
        sepal length in cm  sepal width in cm
record
0              NaN                3.5
1              4.9                3.0
2              NaN                3.2
3              4.6                3.1
4              5.0                3.6
```

Finding and removing missing values

Missing data can plague single cells or entire rows of data, often in a manner silent to the practitioner. Therefore, tools are required to hunt down the missing values, count them, and remove or replace them. This is another area where pandas shines with built-in functions to make your life easier. As mentioned earlier, pandas fills the missing values in a DataFrame with the `NaN` null character. Once data is loaded into a DataFrame, you can find all the null values with the `.isnull()` method. Most datasets are too large to look through the output cell by cell, so pandas also provides a derived method to check whether any missing records exist and, if so, to count them. The derived methods are as follows:

- `.isnull().values.any()`
- `.isnull().values.sum()`

These pandas methods can work on an entire DataFrame or specific columns, depending on your desired workflow. We will focus on a single column in our examples for the ease of demonstration.

Let's start this section by searching for the missing values and finding out how many there are:

```
# get boolean (True/False) response for each datapoint for NaNs
df['sepal length in cm'].isnull()

# check if any missing values in column
print(df['sepal length in cm'].isnull().values.any())

# # get number of many missing values in column
print(df['sepal length in cm'].isnull().values.sum())
```

You will see the following output after executing the preceding code:

```
True
6
```

This tells us that we do indeed have some missing values in the `sepal length` column and that there are a total of 6 empty cells in that column.

We can replace the missing values with a value of our choice. For demonstration purposes, let's simply put the string value example in the empty cells:

```
# fill missing values with new values, store in new "df_example" dataframe
df_example = df['sepal length in cm'].fillna('example')
print(df_example.head())
```

You will see the following output after executing the preceding code:

```
record
0    example
1        4.9
2    example
3        4.6
4          5
Name: sepal length in cm, dtype: object
```

We can also easily drop the rows or columns with missing values if we don't desire to replace them:

```
# drop rows with missing data
df_dropped = df.dropna(axis=0)
print(df_dropped.head())
```

You will see the following output after executing the preceding code:

record	sepal length in cm	sepal width in cm
1	4.9	3.0
3	4.6	3.1
4	5.0	3.6
6	4.6	3.4
7	5.0	3.4

Notice how the 0,2, and 5 records are now missing; this is because these rows were dropped. We can also drop columns in a similar fashion, as follows:

```
# drop columns with missing data
df_dropped = df.dropna(axis=1)
```

Imputing to replace the missing values

In the case of intermittent missing values, you can predict the replacement values for the empty cells. The mathematical apparatus for predicting these values is called an imputor. Scikit-learn has a built-in method called SimpleImputer(); it is very easy to use the method with these two arguments:

- missing_values = refers to the form of the missing values in your data (for example, nan, 0, or n/a).
- strategy = refers to the impute method (the choices are mean, median, most frequent, and constant).

If you pass strategy = constant, then you can use the fill_value optional argument to pass your constant.

Now, let's import the SimpleImputer module and instantiate the imputer object. We will pass the missing_values = np.nan and strategy = mean args, as follows:

```
# import imputer module from Scikit-learn and instantiate imputer object
from sklearn.impute import SimpleImputer
imputer = SimpleImputer(missing_values=np.nan, strategy='mean')

#define columns to impute on
cols = ['sepal length in cm',
        'sepal width in cm',
        'petal length in cm',
        'petal width in cm',]
```

Next, we will fit the imputer and transform the input data, and store it in a new DataFrame called `df_new`:

```
# fit imputer and transform dataset, store in df_new
out_imp = imputer.fit_transform(df[cols])
df_new = pd.DataFrame(data = out_imp, columns = cols)
df_new = pd.concat([df_new, df[['species']]], axis = 1)
print(df_new.head())
```

You will see the following output after executing the preceding code:

	sepal length in cm	sepal width in cm
0	5.870139	3.5
1	4.900000	3.0
2	5.870139	3.2
3	4.600000	3.1
4	5.000000	3.6

The 0 and 2 records are now imputed values, chosen as the mean of the `sepal length` column.

Feature scaling

A mathematical property is considered to be **scale-invariant** if it does not change when multiplying specified inputs by a constant. For instance, the shape of a curve is invariant to the size of the input lengths. If you require more convincing, picture a distribution with a negative skew (as shown in the *Summary statistics* section of `Chapter 2`, *Basic Terminology and Our End-to-End Example*). Now, multiply the whole distribution by the constant 3. The shape of the distribution or curve does not change, as it remains negatively skewed.

Scaling is important for transformation and learning algorithms that are not scale-invariant. Two examples of algorithms that lack scale-invariance are **principal component analysis** (**PCA**) and *penalized regression*. If you are not familiar with these methods, don't worry as they are covered later in the book. In these cases, large values dominate the parameter space inside the algorithm. The outcome is that a few features (usually the ones on the largest scales) end up having undue influence on the outcome of the mining analysis. The correction strategy is to put each feature on a similar scale, thus allowing downstream methods to focus on variance and skews instead of scale. The most common methods for correcting scale are **normalization** and **standardization**.

Many other scaling methods exist and, if you are curious, you can read Scitkit-learn's published example that compares multiple scalers is available at `https://scikit-learn.org/stable/auto_examples/preprocessing/plot_all_scaling.html`.

Take a moment to digest my quote – *"Thus allowing downstream methods to focus on variance and skews instead of scale."* Variance and skew are properties of the distribution of data (see the *Summary statistics* section of `Chapter 2`, *Basic Terminology and Our End-to-End Example*). Scale is arbitrary but the distribution is not. If you need to be convinced, try experimenting by multiplying an entire dataset by a large constant value. You will find that the data is now on a larger scale, but the shape (that is, distribution) has not changed.

We will return to the iris dataset for this section; let's now load it and define the columns to scale:

```
# load iris dataset
df = pd.read_csv("./data/iris.csv")
df.index.name = "record"

# define columns to scale
cols = ['sepal length in cm',
        'sepal width in cm',
        'petal length in cm',
        'petal width in cm']
```

Normalization

Normalization is used to rescale each feature space so that all values fall between 0 and 1 (or, alternatively, between -1 and 1). There are multiple ways to carry out normalization, but the most common method is the routine that is coded into scikit-learn's `MinMaxScaler()` function. Here is the equation for this normalization method:

Min-Max Normalization

$$x_{i,scaled} = \frac{x_{i,original} - min_Y}{max_Y - min_Y}$$

Where:

x_i = datapoint

Y = column where x resides

Note how there is nothing to protect this transformation from outliers. You will have to remove them before you normalize, otherwise, the relevant points will not be stretched across the full [0-1] range, and the useful data will be "squished" into a smaller range.

Scikit-learn's normalization object is straightforward to use, as demonstrated in the following code:

```
# load module and instantiate scaler object
from sklearn.preprocessing import MinMaxScaler
scaler = MinMaxScaler()

# normalize the data and store in out_scaled numpy array
out_scaled = scaler.fit_transform(df[cols])
```

Standardization

Standardization is used to put the variation within each feature space on the same scale. It does so by spreading the data across the unit variance and centering it at 0. Other values can be chosen for advanced standardization, but variance=1 and mean=0 are the most common.

There is no cap on the minimum or maximum values of standardized data, which makes it relatively robust to outliers and leaves them identifiable after the transformation. Furthermore, scikit-learn has a robust_scale method for even more robustness by using the interquartile range to measure variation instead of standard deviation. For this reason, I recommend using standardization as your main rescale method as opposed to normalization.

Scikit-learn's standardization object is straightforward to use, as demonstrated in the following code:

```
# load module and instantiate scaler object
from sklearn.preprocessing import StandardScaler
scaler = StandardScaler()

# standardize the data and store in out_scaled numpy array
out_scaled = scaler.fit_transform(df[cols])
```

Handling categorical data

Most data mining and machine learning methods are built for continuous variables and integer inputs. They are not built for strings or categorical data, that is, at least not directly. So, part of the data conditioning process is to encode categorical data into something akin to a proxy for continuous data. For more background, variable types are introduced in `Chapter 2`, *Basic Terminology and Our End-to-End Example.*

One consideration to be aware of is whether the variable is ordered or not. For example, an athlete's shoe size is categorical and **ordinal** because the larger shoe size does indicate a larger value, whereas the shoe color is categorical, but not ordinal because one color is not necessarily larger in value than another. In the latter case, we call these variables **nominal.** This section will introduce basic **ordinal encoding** and a strategy called **one-hot encoding,** which is commonly used for both ordinal and nominal variables. It will end with a simple **label encoding** section for converting categorical target variables into something useful in a short, single step.

Before we begin the section, let's load our small example long jump dataset, as follows:

```
# load example long jump dataset
df = pd.read_csv("./data/long_jump.csv")
df.set_index('Person', inplace=True)
```

Ordinal encoding

Ordinal variables have an order to them. Our examples from the long jump dataset are `Jersey Size` and `Shoe Size`. With both of these variables, larger entries mean larger values in an ordered manner. That is, *large* is always bigger than *medium*, which is, in turn, always bigger than *small*. Moreover, these relationships among entries are actually representative of ordered relationships in the real world.

Let's start our example by focusing in on the ordinal 'Jersey Size' and 'Shoe Size' categorical variables in our dateset. We will filter them in as follows:

```
# filter in categorical columns ("cats") for demonstration
cats = ['Jersey Size', 'Shoe Size']
print(df[cats])
```

You will see the following output after executing the preceding code:

```
               Jersey Size  Shoe Size
Person
Thomas              small          7
Jane               medium         10
Vaughn              large         12
Vera               medium          9
Vincent             large         12
Lei-Ann             small          7
```

Now, we will use scikit-learn's **OrdinalEncoder** module to encode our ordinal columns. As always, we will start by importing the relevant module and instantiating the encoder object. We then fit it to our input data and then transform it with the `.fit_transform()` method in a single step. Finally, we will print out the new categories and the resulting transformed array with the `.categories_` call and the `out_enc` print call:

```
# import module and instantiate enc object
from sklearn.preprocessing import OrdinalEncoder
enc = OrdinalEncoder()

# fit and transform in one call and print categories
out_enc = enc.fit_transform(df[cats])
print('identified categories:')
print(enc.categories_)
print('encoded data:')
print(out_enc)
```

You will see the following output after executing the preceding code:

```
identified categories:
[array(['large', 'medium', 'small'], dtype=object), array([7, 9, 10, 12], dtype=object)]
encoded data:
[[2. 0.]
 [1. 2.]
 [0. 3.]
 [1. 1.]
 [0. 3.]
 [2. 0.]]
```

For the first feature (`'Jersey Size'`), the available categories are *-ordered list-* [`'large'`, `'medium'`, `'small'`], and for the second feature (`'Shoe Size'`), the available categories are *-ordered list-* [`7`, `9`, `10`, `12`]. The output array is printed next. You should be able to map the input data to the output data using the preceding two ordered lists. Make sure that you can reconcile this encoding transformation before moving on.

Next, we will simply overwrite the original columns in our DataFrame with the newly-encoded continuous features:

```
# overwrite categorical features in original dataframe
df[cats] = out_enc
print(df.head())
```

You will see the following output after executing the preceding code:

	Age	Height	Weight	Jersey Color	Jersey Size	Shoe Size	Long Jump
Person							
Thomas	12	57.5	73.4	blue	2.0	0.0	19.2
Jane	13	65.5	85.3	green	1.0	2.0	25.1
Vaughn	17	71.9	125.9	green	0.0	3.0	14.3
Vera	14	65.3	100.5	red	1.0	1.0	18.3
Vincent	18	70.1	110.7	blue	0.0	3.0	21.1

One-hot encoding

The one-hot technique emerged from the electronics field as a way to record the state of a machine by using simple binary methods (that is, 0's and 1's). The idea is to define one flag for each possible state of the machine, and then have the machine flip the flag that matches its current state to 1, and leave all the other flags at 0. Statisticians have adopted this technique for representing categorical variables in data mining and machine learning. A flag (that is, a new feature) is defined for each possible value of the original feature column and is flipped to 1 if the record is in that state, leaving the remaining flags at 0.

The easiest way to understand the one-hot technique is by seeing it in action. The following table demonstrates one-hot encoding of the categorical feature, **Shoe Size**. The source column includes values 7, **9**, **10**, and **12**. Four possible values mean that there are four new flags and four new feature columns. Additionally, we can use the intuitive names **Shoe Size_7**, **Shoe Size_9**, and so on. The 0's and 1's are then filled in for each row (that is, for each **Person**) recording their state. It is a good idea to study this table carefully before moving on:

One-hot Encoding Example

Source			Encoded				
Person	**Shoe Size**		**Person**	**Shoe Size_7**	**Shoe Size_9**	**Shoe Size_10**	**Shoe Size_12**
Thomas	7		Thomas	1	0	0	0
Jane	10		Jane	0	0	1	0
Vaughn	12		Vaughn	0	0	0	1
Vera	9		Vera	0	1	0	0
Vincent	12		Vincent	0	0	0	1
Lei-Ann	7		Lei-Ann	1	0	0	0

One-hot encoding is confusing to many newcomers, but it is vital that you understand it. For instance, the most popular classifiers in downstream predictions are tree-based methods, and one-hot encoding is considered to be the state-of-the-art solution for categorical input to these methods. Tree-based methods will be introduced in `Chapter 6`, *Prediction with Regression and Classification*.

A significant shortcoming of one-hot encoding is its inability to extrapolate new states that aren't available in the source. In our example, there is no way to define a state of having **Shoe Size=11** since we have no examples of size 11 in our source. This has a cascade effect, essentially limiting any downstream analyses' ability to access the **Shoe Size=11** state.

For our example, we will use the same long jump dataset and `cats` list that we previously loaded in the *Ordinal encoding* section. Let's import the `OneHotEncoder` module and instantiate the `encoder` object. Next, we will fit and transform the variables in the `cats` list. Then, we will use scikit-learn's `.get_feature_next()` method to retrieve the new column names and print them for a sanity check:

```
# import module and instantiate enc object
from sklearn.preprocessing import OneHotEncoder
enc = OneHotEncoder(sparse=False)

# fit and transform in one call and print categories
out_enc = enc.fit_transform(df[cats])
new_cols = enc.get_feature_names(cats).tolist()
print(new_cols)
```

You will see the following output after executing the preceding code:

```
['Jersey Size_large', 'Jersey Size_medium', 'Jersey Size_small', 'Shoe
Size_7', 'Shoe Size_9', 'Shoe Size_10', 'Shoe Size_12']
```

This output matches what we expected. We have a new feature column for each flag needed to represent the state possibilities of the dataset, and they are named intuitively such as `Jersey Size_medium` and `Shoe Size_10`.

Now, all that's left is to replace the source columns with the new one-hot features. We can do this by concatenating a temporary DataFrame with the source, after dropping the original columns in the `cats` list:

```
# create temporary dataframe "df_enc" for concatenation with original data
df_enc = pd.DataFrame(data = out_enc, columns = new_cols)
df_enc.index = df.index

# drop original columns and concat new encoded columns
df.drop(cats, axis=1, inplace=True)
df = pd.concat([df, df_enc], axis = 1)
print(df.columns)
```

You will see the following output after executing the preceding code:

```
Index(['Age', 'Height', 'Weight', 'Training Hours/week', 'Jersey Color',
       'Long Jump', 'Jersey Size_large', 'Jersey Size_medium',
       'Jersey Size_small', 'Shoe Size_7', 'Shoe Size_9', 'Shoe Size_10',
       'Shoe Size_12'])
```

Label encoding

Often, the only column that needs encoding is the label or output column. For these situations, scikit-learn includes the simple `LabelEncoder` module that encodes a single column. It works on integer and string inputs; the following code example demonstrates both of these cases:

```
# import modules and instantiate enc object
from sklearn import preprocessing
enc = preprocessing.LabelEncoder()

# fit with integer labels and transform
out_enc = enc.fit_transform([1, 2, 5, 2, 4, 2, 5])
print(out_enc)

# fit with string labels and transform
out_enc = enc.fit_transform(["blue", "red", "blue", "green", "red", "red"])
print(out_enc)
```

You will see the following output after executing the preceding code:

```
[0 1 3 1 2 1 3]
[0 2 0 1 2 2]
```

High-dimensional data

Often when data mining, an analyst is happy to get their hands on a new feature column because the hope is that this added feature will bring additional new information. While this expectation fits with human intuition, there is an enormous caveat that must be understood and respected. This caveat is a result of what's known as the **curse of dimensionality**, which was coined in the 1950s by the mathematician, Richard E. Bellman. In short, a statistically-significant representation of chunks of feature space requires exponentially more and more examples (that is, rows) as the number of dimensions (that is, features) grows. Failure to grow the number of examples with the number of dimensions causes the dataset to become sparse and no longer representative of ground truth. The common rule of thumb is that you should have five examples for every one dimension. Based on my experience, I recommend increasing this ratio to 10-to-1, if possible.

Dimension reduction

Due to the curse of dimensionality, a reduction of the number of feature columns is sometimes required before you can get any work done. However, there are also other reasons for reducing the dimensions. For example, plotting and visualizing scatter data on a two-dimensional piece of paper or computer screen requires that you have only two dimensions to show.

There are two main strategies for reducing dimensions, as follows:

- **Selection**: Choose the best features and eliminate the others.
- **Transformation**: Create new features that summarize the combinations of the original ones.

Feature selection

Feature selection is done with two overarching strategies. The first is with **feature filtering**, which seeks to define an important measurement, and then filter in only the most important. The second is with **wrapper methods**, which seek to mimic downstream work and sample different combinations of features before choosing the best results.

In other words, wrapper methods build mini-models with subsets of features and score the ones that perform the best.

Feature filtering

Feature filtering is simple at its core; your goal is to find a way to score importance, and then keep only the most important. Of course, the devil is in the details and there is more than one way to score importance. The most common methods are defining a **variance threshold** and sorting by a **correlation coefficient.**

The variance threshold

As the name suggests, the variance threshold method works by setting a threshold value and removing the features that are below this value. You can refer to the *Summary statistics* section of `Chapter 2`, *Basic Terminology and Our End-to-End Example*, for a description of variance. The `VarianceThreshold` object in scikit-learn stores the variances for each feature upon fitting, so I recommend you prefit first to take advantage of this feature. Remember to prefit with no threshold, so that all the features are kept after the prefit.

A good workflow to use is as follows:

1. Prefit with no threshold.
2. Analyze the variances.
3. Choose the threshold.
4. Refit with the chosen threshold.

Let's start by loading the iris dataset and defining the input columns that we want to select from:

```
# load iris dataset
df = pd.read_csv("iris.csv"); df.index.name = 'record'

# define columns to filter
cols = ['sepal length in cm',
        'sepal width in cm',
        'petal length in cm',
        'petal width in cm',]
```

Now, we can instantiate the VarianceThreshold object, prefit it with no threshold, and then analyze it. You will see the following output after executing the preceding code:

```
# instantiate Scikit-learn object with no threshold
from sklearn.feature_selection import VarianceThreshold
selector = VarianceThreshold()

# prefit object with df[cols]
selector.fit(df[cols])

# check feature variances before selection
print(selector.variances_)
```

You will see the following output after executing the preceding code:

```
[0.68  0.19  3.09  0.58]
```

For demonstration purposes, we will choose 0.6 as the threshold and then refit. From the output, you should expect columns 0 and 2 (0.68 and 3.09) to be selected:

```
# set threshold into selector object
selector.set_params(threshold=1.0)

# refit and transform, store output in out_sel
out_sel = selector.fit_transform(df[cols])

# check which features were chosen
print(selector.get_support())
```

You will see the following output after executing the preceding code:

```
[ True False True False]
```

Now, we can apply the filtering using the scikit-learn get_support() method:

```
# filter in the selected features
df_sel = df.iloc[:, selector.get_support()]

# add labels to new dataframe and sanity check
df_sel = pd.concat([df_sel, df[['species']]], axis = 1)
print(df_sel.head())
```

You will see the following output after executing the preceding code:

```
        sepal length in cm  petal length in cm species
record
0                      5.1                 1.4  setosa
1                      4.9                 1.4  setosa
2                      4.7                 1.3  setosa
3                      4.6                 1.5  setosa
4                      5.0                 1.4  setosa
```

The correlation coefficient

In mathematics, correlation refers to the strength of the agreement between two variables. **Pearson's** *r* coefficient is the most commonly-used correlation metric. The values, *-1* and *1*, indicate the largest agreement or highest **negative** or **positive correlation**, respectively. Values close to 0 indicate a low correlation between the two variables. You can use pandas' built-in .corr() method and Seaborn's **heatmap** to visually analyze many *r* coefficients at once, and then filter in the features with the highest correlation to your output.

We will start our example by loading the low-level Python-plotting matplotlib library, so that Seaborn has access to its color maps on the heatmap. Let's then load the boston dataset, as follows:

```
# import matplotlib for access to color maps
import matplotlib.pyplot as plt

# load boston dataset
from sklearn.datasets import load_boston
dataset = load_boston()
df = pd.DataFrame(dataset.data, columns=dataset.feature_names)
df['MEDV'] = dataset.target; df.index.name = 'record'
```

Now, let's use pandas' .corr() method to find the *r* coefficient for all the variables' pairings. We can then plot using the Seaborn heatmap routine and set the color map to matplotlib's Blues:

```
# find correlation with pandas ".corr()"
cor = df.corr()

# visualize with Seaborn heat map, color map = Blues
sns.heatmap(cor, annot=False, cmap=plt.cm.Blues)
plt.show()
```

You will see the following output after executing the preceding code:

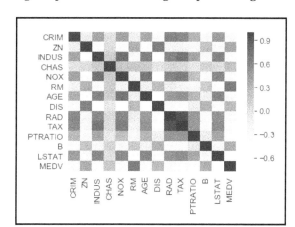

The scale on the right side of the preceding diagram should help to guide your eyes as you analyze the heatmap. A darker blue means a darker correlation. Notice that the diagonals are all r=1 because they paired with themselves. You can use this method to quickly check for correlations. This heatmap is particularly convenient if you have multiple output variables to analyze at once, or if you are looking for highly correlated variables. We only have a single output variable ('MEDV') in this dataset, so let's zoom in on that and check the *r* coefficients of this output paired with each input:

```
# get correlation values with target variable
cor_target = abs(cor['MEDV'])
print(cor_target)
```

You will see the following output after executing the preceding code:

```
CRIM       0.385832
ZN         0.360445
INDUS      0.483725
CHAS       0.175260
NOX        0.427321
RM         0.695360
AGE        0.376955
DIS        0.249929
RAD        0.381626
TAX        0.468536
PTRATIO    0.507787
B          0.333461
LSTAT      0.737663
MEDV       1.000000
Name: MEDV, dtype: float64
```

For demonstration purposes, we will choose `0.6` as the threshold and then filter. From the output, you should expect columns 5 and 12 (0.69 and 0.74) to be selected:

```
# choose features above threshold 0.6
selected_cols = cor_target[cor_target>0.6]
print("selected columns, correlation with target > 0.6")
print(selected_cols)
# filter in the selected features
df_sel = df[selected_cols.index]
print(df_sel.head())
```

You will see the following output after executing the preceding code:

```
selected columns, correlation with target > 0.6
RM         0.695360
LSTAT      0.737663
MEDV       1.000000
Name: MEDV, dtype: float64
           RM  LSTAT  MEDV
record
0        6.575   4.98  24.0
1        6.421   9.14  21.6
2        7.185   4.03  34.7
3        6.998   2.94  33.4
4        7.147   5.33  36.2
```

Wrapper methods

A **wrapper method** invokes a machine learning prediction algorithm and scores the contribution of each feature to a good prediction. The **sequential** version then updates the feature list with each iteration of the algorithm fitting. You can do this in the **forward** or **backward** directions, meaning that you can start with zero features selected and add one or more in each iteration, or you can start with all the available features and whittle them away in each iteration.

Sequential feature selection

Sequential feature selection can work in the forward or backward direction, giving rise to the obviously named routines: **forward sequential selection** and **backward sequential selection**. Usually, when practitioners use this terminology, they are referring to a routine where they decide the score function and update the strategy (that is, add or remove features) themselves – by writing custom code to perform. Luckily, if you are willing to use the prediction algorithm's automatic scoring, scikit-learn has a built-in method called **recursive feature elimination** (**RFE**).

Scikit-learn's RFE method works with any prediction algorithm object that has a `.coef_` or `.feature_importances_` attribute in the fit object. There are quite a few candidate algorithms to choose from, but I recommend `LinearRegression()` for continuous target variables, and `RandomForestClassifier()` for categorical target variables.

For this example, let's start by defining the feature columns that we want to select from, as follows:

```
# load iris dataset
df = pd.read_csv("./data/iris.csv"); df.index.name = 'record'

# define columns to select from
cols = ['sepal length in cm',
        'sepal width in cm',
        'petal length in cm',
        'petal width in cm',]
```

We will use the support vector machine classifier (SVC) as the estimator for our example RFE. Now, let's import our modules and define the independent (X) and dependent (y) variables for the SVC object:

```
# load modules for RFE and the classifier SVC
from sklearn.feature_selection import RFE
from sklearn.svm import SVC

# set independent vars to X and dependent var to y
X = df[cols]
y = df['species']
```

Next, we will instantiate both the RFE and SVC object, and pass the SVC object as an argument into RFE. We will use the `n_features_to_select` arg to choose the number of output features (2, in this case). Then, we fit and check the feature rankings with RFE's `ranking_` attribute, as follows:

```
# Create the RFE object and rank each pixel
svc = SVC(kernel="linear", C=1)
rfe = RFE(estimator=svc, n_features_to_select=2, step=1)
rfe.fit(X, y)

# print rankings
print(cols)
print(rfe.ranking_)
```

You will see the following output after executing the preceding code:

```
['sepal length', 'sepal width', 'petal length', 'petal width']
[3 2 1 1]
```

The chosen attributes are given the importance of 1. Since we passed `n_features_to_select = "2"` as an arg to the `RFE` object, it chooses two features. In this case, it's selected `"petal length"` and `"petal width"`.

Transformation

A common strategy for reducing data dimensions is **transformation**. This strategy chooses a few new dimensions, or feature vectors, to project the original data into. You can think of this as a rotation of the data to point in a more helpful direction. Of course, the trick is in how you choose these new feature vector directions. There are two common mathematical methods, both of which are fully deterministic and targeted at either the **supervised** or **unsupervised** case. The supervised version includes labels on the data, while the unsupervised version does not. Let's use a small example to explain transformations and help you build some intuition about the methods.

- **Rotation example**: Imagine that you're holding your hand up in front of an overhead projector asking an observer to identify what they see. Now, imagine rotating your hand in all different directions. Some angles and positions are more helpful than others. For instance, sometimes your hand will look like a tall rectangle or a rotated plane, and at other times, it will look like a paper turkey from grade school. The data (that is, your hand) has not changed but you've altered the effectiveness of a downstream analysis (that is, from the observer) by merely rotating.

- **New feature vector selection**: Let's continue using our example of the hand and projector:

  - **Unsupervised**: We don't have labels, so our goal should be to expose as much information as possible. Holding your hand normally to the projector beam will maximize the surface area of your shadow, so this will be a good direction to choose. In data mining, we use mathematics to find the direction that maximizes information in the form of feature variance. We then rotate the data into this high-variance (that is, high-information) space. For more information, see the *PCA* section in this chapter.

- **Supervised**: We have labels and can use them to our advantage. Let's label the thumb with "0" and all the other fingers with "1". Now, in your head, draw a circle around your "0" label item (that is, thumb) and a larger one around all of your "1" items. Mark the center of each circle and then rotate your hand until those two centers are as far apart as possible, along a line. You've found the line that discriminates the two class labels ("0" and "1") maximally. For more information, see the *Linear Discriminant Analysis (LDA)* section in this chapter.

PCA

PCA is used to reduce the dimensions of data in an unsupervised manner. The method's goal is to identify new feature vectors, maximize the variance in the data, and then project the original data into this new space. Please revisit the short example in the previous section for an intuitive description.

The new feature vectors that maximize variance are called **eigenvectors**, and are the principal components. There is one component for each original feature. The power of this method comes when you drop the less important ones and keep only those with the most informative content, thus lowering the dimensions. Scikit-learn has an `explained_variance_` attribute that can be used to rank the importance of each principal component. More commonly in data mining, you will use the `n_components` arg to specify a new, lowered number of dimensions and allow scikit-learn to sort by variance and drop the features automatically.

In the following PCA example, the raw scatter plot of the iris dataset is on the left. The most variation is captured in the direction of the red arrow (`"PCA1"`), and the runner-up is the orthogonal direction that is captured by the black arrow (`"PCA2"`). Now imagine rotating the dataset so that the two axes are the first two principal components. Finally, study the PCA scatter plot on the right where the axes are the directions, `"PCA1"` and `"PCA2"`:

The connection between the right and left scatters should be clear in your mind before you move on from this section. It's this kind of intuition that will allow you to do powerful analysis while also knowing what the underlying mathematics is doing. The methods in this book are not black boxes, and you should force yourself to learn and understand them. You almost certainly do yourself a disservice as a data mining practitioner otherwise.

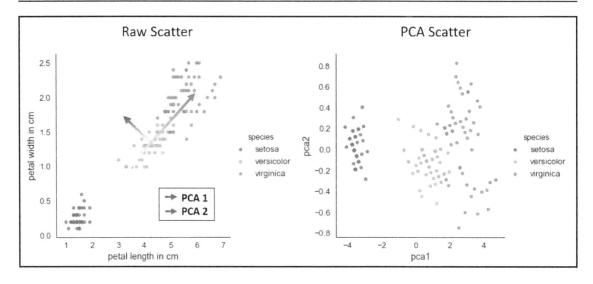

Now, let's take a look at the scikit-learn PCA object, syntax, and the code that is needed to create the preceding scatter plot:

```
# instantiate pca object with 2 output dimensions
from sklearn.decomposition import PCA
pca = PCA(n_components=2)

# fit and transform using 2 input dimensions
out_pca = pca.fit_transform(df[['petal length in cm',
                                'petal width in cm',]])

# create pca output dataframe and add label column "species"
df_pca = pd.DataFrame(data = out_pca, columns = ['pca1', 'pca2'])
df_pca = pd.concat([df_pca, df[['species']]], axis = 1)

# plot scatter of pca data
sns.lmplot(x='pca1', y='pca2', hue='species', data=df_pca, fit_reg=False)
```

The explained variance for each principal component falls off quickly. For instance, even on datasets with 50 to 100 incoming dimensions, it's common practice to keep only 2 or 3 principal components because they often explain greater than 95% of the variance. We can use `explained_variance_ratio` to show the variance content for "PCA1" and "PCA2", as follows:

```
# get variance explained by each component
print(pca.explained_variance_ratio_)
```

You will see the following output after executing the preceding code:

```
[0.99019934 0.00980066]
```

Here, on the iris dataset with two incoming dimensions, the first principal component explains 99.02% of the variance with the second component only explaining 0.01%. This means that almost all the information that you need for data mining is captured by the first principal component. We can visualize this outcome with violins for each component. It's obvious from the following plots which component contains the most helpful and informative content:

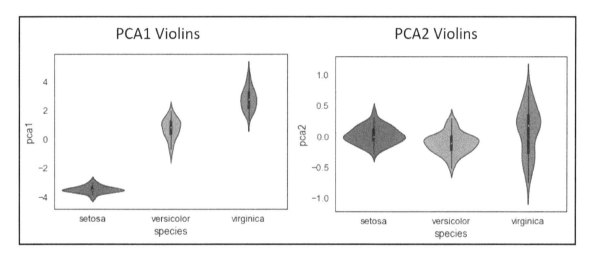

LDA

LDA is used to reduce the dimensions of data in a supervised manner. The method's goal is to identify the average values of each group or class and find the new dimensions that maximally separate or discriminate between the class centers. Then, just as with PCA, the incoming data is rotated and projected into the new space described by the new LDA dimensions. Please revisit the short example in the *Transformation* section for an intuitive description.

The new feature vectors that maximize separation are called **discriminants**. There is one discriminant for each one-versus-all comparison, meaning that there is *n-1*, where *n* is the number of classes.

In the following LDA example, the raw scatter plot of the iris dataset is on the left. Notice that we've chosen different incoming features compared to the PCA example from the previous section. The setosa-versus-all class separation is captured in the direction of the red arrow ("LDA1"), and the versicolor-versus-virginica separation is captured by the black arrow ("LDA2"). Now, imagine rotating the dataset so that the two axes are these two discriminants. Finally, study the LDA scatter plot on the right where the axes are the directions, "LDA1" and "LDA2":

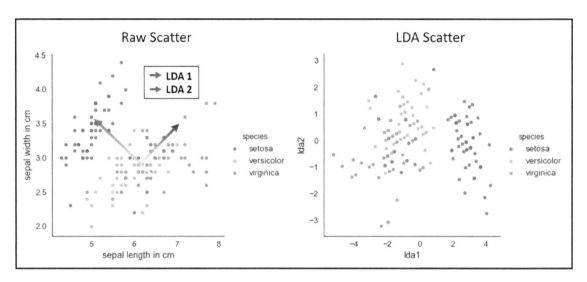

Now, let's take a look at the scikit-learn LDA object, syntax, and the code that is needed to create the preceding scatter plot:

```
# instantiate lda object with 2 output dimensions
from sklearn.discriminant_analysis import LinearDiscriminantAnalysis
lda = LinearDiscriminantAnalysis(n_components=2)

# fit and transform using 2 input dimensions
cols = ['sepal length in cm','sepal width in cm']
lda.fit(df[cols], df['species'])
out_lda = lda.transform(df[cols])

# create lda output dataframe and add label column "species"
df_lda = pd.DataFrame(data = out_lda, columns = ['lda1', 'lda2'])
df_lda = pd.concat([df_lda, df[['species']]], axis = 1)
```

Summary

This chapter covered the basics of data cleanup and dimensionality reduction. After reading it, you should understand how to work with missing values, rescale input data, and handle categorical variables. You should also understand the troubles of having high-dimensional data and how to combat it with feature reduction techniques including filter, wrapper, and transformation methods.

In the next chapter, we will cover clustering and other ways in which to group records for data mining insights.

5
Grouping and Clustering Data

A good way to describe data shape is to assign data points to groups based on similar features and then visualize the groupings. This allows users to put data points into relevant groups and ultimately uncover patterns. In data mining, these groups are called "clusters". This chapter will start with a general background on the topics required to understand common clustering techniques. Following this, it will get into the specifics of a few popular clustering methods and explain how to apply each of them.

The following topics will be covered in this chapter:

- Introducing clustering concepts
- Mean separation (K-means and K-means++)
- Agglomerative clustering (hierarchical clustering)
- Density clustering (DBSCAN)
- Spectral clustering

Introducing clustering concepts

Grouping and clustering methods have a very simple goal, and I want you to keep this goal in mind throughout this entire chapter.

The goal of clustering: Group similar things together, while separating dissimilar things.

That is the beginning and end of the motivation, but of course, as with other data mining tasks, the devil is in the details.

So, let's start the discussion by brainstorming what types of mathematical machinery we will need to get this task done right. We will need a quantitative way to describe the following three things:

1. **Location of group**: A way to define where a group is in space that spans multiple dimensions
2. **Similarity**: What it means to be similar and dissimilar to other data points
3. **Termination Condition**: When to stop grouping, preferably without human intervention

If we can find a way to get these three things defined computationally, then we should be ready to get started with grouping data together into clusters.

In this chapter, I examine a problem (how to cluster), examine the considerations needed to find the solution, and then reconcile the current best known methods with those considerations. I urge you to take this approach on new topics you encounter in the field. Human beings developed these methods, so tracing their thought process is a good way to learn the ins and outs of a new topic. Data mining methods are not black boxes. You can learn them properly. You can do it!

Clustering is like golf. It's very simple, it's just not easy. Let's take a look at how the clustering problem very quickly gets difficult. Take a look at the plot on the right and how the spread of each cluster overlaps with the others. Now, imagine that phenomenon of cluster-overlap happening in 100 dimensions at once (which is not an uncommon number of features in a real-world dataset). Often, clustering is done in an unsupervised environment (that is, without labels), so imagine not having the color-coding on the right-side plot as well. Clustering quickly becomes a very hard problem to solve:

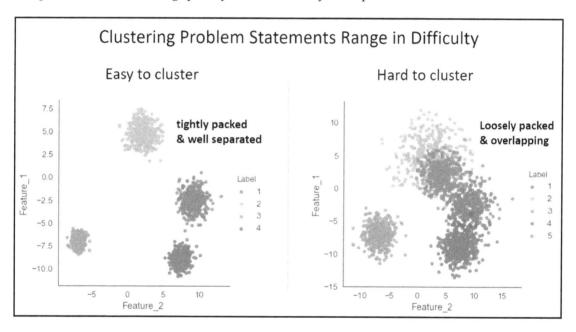

Location of the group

Of course, we don't want to jump in every step of the way and use our human intuition to mark group locations. That would take a long time, and humans are not good at thinking in more than three dimensions. So, we need to quantify this task. The following screenshot demonstrates the two common ways for defining cluster centers (**centroids** and **medioids).** I encourage you to study it before reading the following sections, think about what makes the two center choices different, and then read on and see whether you are correct:

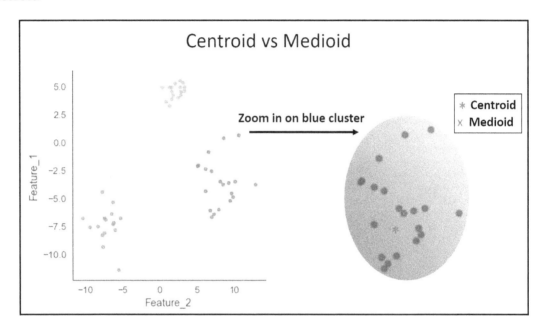

Euclidean space (centroids)

For numerical data in Euclidean space, the most common way to identify the location of a cluster is by finding the mean of its points, which corresponds to its center of mass. This point is called the **centroid**. It is the geometrical center, and is found with a straightforward mean calculation.

Euclidean and non-Euclidean space is defined in the upcoming section, entitled "Similarity", where the distinction is reflected in the resulting equations. For now, you should focus on the topic at hand and try to visualize group location as defined by centroids and medioids, the latter of which are discussed in the next section.

Non-Euclidean space (medioids)

For data in non-Euclidean space, the story gets a bit more complicated. Examples of non-Euclidean space are string comparison features, and mixed data that has both categorical and numerical data. In these cases, a geometrical center does not exist so we need a different strategy. The most common solution is to identify a **medioid** in each cluster. A medioid is the data point that is closest to the other points in the cluster. It *must* be one of the actual data points in the set, and can be thought of as the best representative of that cluster.

 In the field of data mining, medioids of clusters are also known as **clustoids**.

The next logical question is: What do we mean by "closest to the other data points"?

This is for us to define, and there are multiple strategies. First, we decide on a similarity metric between points, then compare each point to every other point based on this similarity metric to see which one is closest to all the others. Different similarity metrics are introduced in the next section. The next obvious question is: How do you define "closest"? It is commonly found by looking for the lowest score on one of the following metrics:

- The maximum distance to other points in cluster
- The mean distance to all other points in cluster
- The sum-of-squares distance to all other points

 Regardless of the metric chosen, finding *medioids* carries a heavy hit to fit time. Every point is compared to every other point in the cluster, so these methods don't scale well. For readers who've studied algorithm design, this calculation scales as $O(n^2)$.

Similarity

Now that we know how to locate our group in space, we need to define what it means to be similar. The metrics explained in this section are the most commonly used ones by practitioners.

 In the field of data mining, similarity metrics are also known as **distance metrics**.

Euclidean space

Euclidean space is something we can visualize easily in our mind. Locations in this space are described by standard vectors and coordinate groupings. As a result, Euclidean similarity metrics are straightforward and intuitive. If you study the equations, you'll see they make sense.

The Euclidean distance

The **Euclidean distance** is something you learned in grade school, even if you didn't realize it. The **Pythagorean theorem** states that $x^2 + y^2 = z^2$, where x and y are lengths of the sides of a right triangle, and z is the length of the hypotenuse. Solve for z over the n number of points and you will get the equation for Euclidean distance. This is also known as the shortest distance between two points or the path traversed "as the crow flies". The Euclidean distance is also called **L2 Norm**:

$$Euclidean\ Distance = \sqrt{\sum_{i=1}^{n} (x_i - y_i)^2}$$

The Manhattan distance

The **Manhattan distance** is best understood by picturing its nicknames the **taxicab metric** and **cityblock distance**. The metric itself measures the distance between two points, given the shape of the grid required to traverse the difference. You can see this in your mind by picturing a taxicab driver turning left and right down the grid of streets and avenues in a downtown area of a big city. This snake-like motion is in stark contrast to the crow's path defined by the Euclidean distance. The Manhattan Distance is also called the **L1 Norm**:

$$Manhattan\ Distance = \sum_{i=1}^{n} |x_i - y_i|$$

Maximum distance

The **Maximum distance** is also named so appropriately that you can automatically intuit what it means at first read. It is the maximum distance between point x_i and the other points in y_i. So, it can be used to answer the question: "How far away is point x_i from the farthest point away in the same cluster?":

$$Maximum\ Distance = max_i\left(|x_i - y_i|\right)$$

Non-Euclidean space

In non-Euclidean space, coordinate systems fall apart. The axes of the system are either curved or disjointed, and cannot be mapped consistently throughout the space. So, the distance between point a and point b would not be the same upon translation, and is therefore meaningless.

You can build one of these spaces at home or simply visualize the following example in your mind:

Let's start with a Euclidean space for comparison. Grab a piece of graph paper (the kind with pre-printed vertical and horizontal lines). Draw a dot at the point located at [17, 9], where the indices are the lines on the paper (horizontal line 17 and vertical column 9) and another at [32,15]. Then, draw a line between the two and calculate the distance between them with the Euclidean distance metric introduced earlier.

Now, let's build a non-Euclidean space. Grab a piece of printer paper with no pre-printed lines and crumple it into a ball. Partially uncrumple the paper so it still has a bowl shape. Then, draw a dot at the point located at [17, 9], where the indices are crinkles on the paper (horizontal crinkle 17 and vertical crinkle 9). Not only is counting the crinkles hard, but they are disjointed and horizontal – crinkle 17 probably doesn't even extend to vertical crinkle 9. Now, focus on the bowl shape in the paper. Even if you could find [17,9] and [32,15], translating them both by the same arbitrary distance across the page changes the distance between them as calculated by Euclidean distance. This is because you've made a **curved space**.

The cosine distance

The issues caused by curved spaces are addressed using the **cosine distance**. The derivation is beyond the scope of this book, but if you have experience with matrix algebra, you can start with the definition of a dot product and back out to the equation as follows:

$$Cosine\ Distance = 1 - \cos(\theta)$$

The Jaccard distance

The **Jaccard distance** is a good example of why this set of equations are called **similarity metrics**. Paul Jaccard's comparison takes two entities (X and Y) and finds the ratio of common attributes over total attributes. In mathematics, these two quantities are called the **intersection** and the **union**, respectively:

$$Jaccard\ Distance = 1 - \frac{X \cap Y}{X \cup Y}$$

$$where\ \cap = intersection,\ and\ \cup = union$$

Termination condition

Before working on a project with multiple moving parts, it's always good practice to define a stopping or termination condition. It's an answer to the question: "What does it mean for the project to be complete? What does the word *done* mean in the current context?"

In this context, we want to call the job done when the correct number of groupings have been found, and when the chosen number of groupings have been defined (for example, location, size, and shape) to the best of our cluster method's ability.

In clustering, "Done" is when the correct number of well-defined clusters are found.

With known number of groupings

Sometimes, finding the number of groupings is easy because the definition of the problem necessarily brings with it a stopping condition; for instance, grouping audio samples from a recorded conversation where you know exactly five people were talking. In this case, the necessary goal would be to find five groups. In data mining we often call these groups "k"s. The mean of the group is the location of the cluster as described by its **centroid**, and is the method used by the **k-means** algorithm. If the correct *k* value is known, then the termination condition focuses on **convergence** of an appropriate quality score. Convergence simply means that further fitting doesn't change the quality at all, and of course there is no reason to keep going at that point.

Without known number of groupings

A value for *k* is not always known a priori. The most common approach in these situations is to build a math routine that stops creating clusters at the point when the next inclusion would make a bad cluster. The approach is to again define cluster quality based on what's important to your problem statement, then combine these into clusters until the quality score falls precipitously, in which case you've reached your stopping condition.

Quality score and silhouette score

Practitioners use diameter, radius, or density calculations as inputs for measures of quality. The total distance between all points within a cluster is typically termed **cohesion**, while the total distance between clusters is termed **separation**. The most popular quality score is called the **silhouette coefficient (S)** and is a balance of cohesion and separation. For a point *i*, if *a* is the average distance to all other points within its own cluster, and *b* is average distance to all points in nearest neighboring cluster, the silhouette coefficient is given by the following formula:

$$S_i = \frac{(b_i - a_i)}{max(a_i, b_i)}$$

The term *max(a,b)* simply means "take the maximum of the two values a and b". A useful summary score for cluster quality is the average silhouette coefficient across all points, known as the **silhouette score (S_{ave})**. For *n* points, the silhouette score is given by the following formula:

$$silhouette\ score = mean(S_n)$$

Silhouette scores range between [-1,1] with larger scores corresponding to better cluster quality. Study the following screenshot to gain intuition on using the silhouette score as a measure of cluster quality. It shows poor cluster quality on the left and good cluster quality on the right:

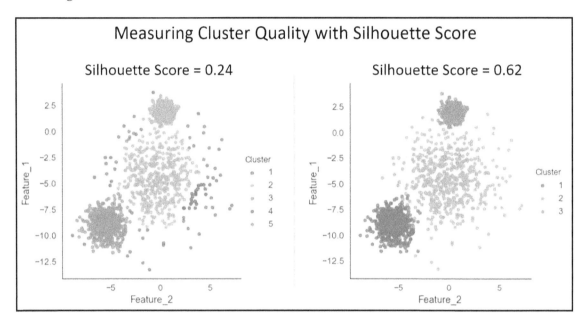

Scikit-learn has a built-in `silhouette_samples` function for finding the coefficient for each data point, and `silhouette_score` for finding the average score across the whole dataset. Some example code is as follows:

```
from sklearn import metrics
S_i = metrics.silhouette_samples(X, cluster_labels)
S = metrics.silhouette_score(X, cluster_labels)
```

Clustering methods

The clustering methods in scikit-learn have a nice congruent usage that, for the most part, matches the following pseudocode across all the algorithms:

```
### this is pseudocode. it will not execute ###
# import module and instantiate method object
from sklearn.cluster import Method
clus = Method(args*)
```

```
# fit to input data
clus.fit(X_input)

# get cluster assignments of X_input
X_assigned = clus.labels_
```

The rest of this chapter will cover some common methods used for data clustering. The following is a group of plots comparing different cluster methods and how they assign data points into groups:

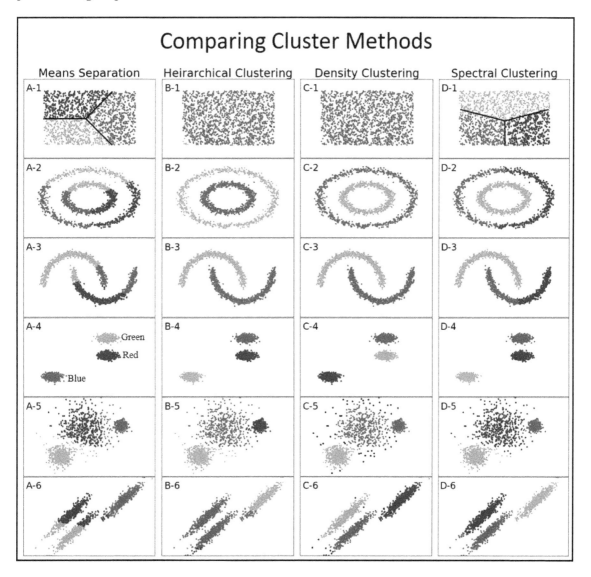

Take a minute to study the preceding "Comparing Cluster Methods" screenshot and look for any qualitative trends or patterns before reading the following sections. Your goal should be to read the rest of the chapter looking for validation of your qualitative pattern recognition. Trust me, if you take this approach you will gain intuition quickly.

Let's build a function that creates a demonstration dataset of blobs for clustering examples. You can call this function and use the resulting set of blobs to run the code in the rest of the chapter:

```
# import datasets module from Sci-kit learn
from sklearn import datasets

# function to create data for clustering examples
def make_blobs():
    # build blobs for demonstration
    n_samples = 1500
    blobs = datasets.make_blobs(n_samples=n_samples,
                                centers=5,
                                cluster_std=[3.0, 0.9, 1.9, 1.9, 1.3],
                                random_state=51)
    # create a Pandas dataframe for the data
    df = pd.DataFrame(blobs[0], columns=['Feature_1', 'Feature_2'])
    df.index.name = 'record'
    return df

df = make_blobs()
print(df.head())

# plot scatter of blob set
sns.lmplot(x='Feature_2', y='Feature_1',
           data=df, fit_reg=False)
```

You will see the following output on the execution of the preceding code:

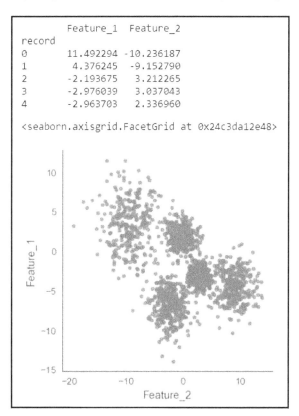

```
        Feature_1  Feature_2
record
0       11.492294  -10.236187
1        4.376245   -9.152790
2       -2.193675    3.212265
3       -2.976039    3.037043
4       -2.963703    2.336960

<seaborn.axisgrid.FacetGrid at 0x24c3da12e48>
```

Means separation

One way to cluster is to define a group by its centroid and keep moving them until convergence. Yes, it is really that simple! In order to use this method, however, you must know the number of clusters (k) at fit time. In other words, you have to tell the algorithm how many clusters to find, or it will not work.

K-means

The basic method of means separation is called **K-means clustering**. It is the simplest and most widely used method in the field of data mining. The family of variants and enhancements on the base method is growing everyday, but at its core it is only four steps:

1. Pick the *k* initial cluster centers at random from points in the input data
2. Assign all the data points to the cluster to which they are closest to
3. Move the *k* centroids to the center of all the points inside the newly created clusters
4. Repeat until *k* clusters stop changing (for example, convergence)

This method uses centroids to define location, Euclidean distance as similarity metric, and cohesion as the quality score. Termination occurs when the quality score converges, as measured by a change to less than the **tolerance** amount. The **K-means++** and **mini batch** variants in the K-means family are introduced later in the section.

What should you notice from the "Comparing Cluster Methods" screenshot: The K-means fit algorithm treats clusters as spherical in nature; in other words, it carries the assumption of Gaussian decay of the distribution. When this assumption breaks down, it has a hard time. See boxes A-2 and A-3 and focus on the blue cluster. Blue assignments spill into what should be green or red because the fit simply groups with a 2D circle emanating from the centroid. Notice how, for example, there is a large gap between the sets of points assigned blue. If K-means had a density or connection component, the blue assignments would not span this gap because the density is zero in the gap, and there are obviously no points close enough to be considered connected either. These are some of the main motivations for the development of the density clustering and spectral clustering methods, which will be introduced later in the chapter.

Notable args for cluster object: Set the tolerance with the `tol` arg when you instantiate the K-means cluster object. You can use `max_iter` to force a stop if the tolerance value is not met after some large number of fit iterations.

An example of applying K-means in Scikit-learn is included in the following code:

```
# generate blob example dataset
df = make_blobs()

# import module and instantiate K-means object
from sklearn.cluster import KMeans
clus = KMeans(n_clusters=5, tol=0.004, max_iter=300)

# fit to input data
clus.fit(df)
```

```
# get cluster assignments of input data and print first five labels
df['K-means Cluster Labels'] = clus.labels_
print(df['K-means Cluster Labels'][:5].tolist())
```

You will see the following output on the execution of the preceding code:

```
[3, 3, 1, 1, 1]
```

Now, let's use Seaborn's scatter plot to visualize the grouping of a blob set with the cluster labels displayed:

```
sns.lmplot(x='Feature_2', y='Feature_1',
           hue="K-means Cluster Labels", data=df, fit_reg=False)
```

You will see the following output on the execution of the preceding code:

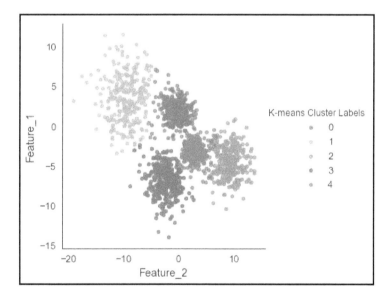

Finding *k*

Of course, with many data mining problem statements, the value for *k* is not known a priori. The most common method for finding *k* is to choose an appropriate quality score (one that matches your problem statement) and then fit different values of *k* to find the best score. In my work, I most often use the silhouette score as the default method. Let's look at the code for finding *k*:

```
# generate blob example dataset
df = make_blobs()
```

```
# find best value for k using silhouette score
# import metrics module
from sklearn import metrics

# create list of k values to test and then use for loop
n_clusters = [2,3,4,5,6,7,8]
for k in n_clusters:
    kmeans = KMeans(n_clusters=k, random_state=42).fit(df)
    cluster_labels = kmeans.predict(df)
    S = metrics.silhouette_score(df, cluster_labels)
    print("n_clusters = {:d}, silhouette score {:1f}".format(k, S))
```

You will see the following output on the execution of the preceding code:

```
n_clusters = 2, silhouette score 0.442473
n_clusters = 3, silhouette score 0.442798
n_clusters = 4, silhouette score 0.513624
n_clusters = 5, silhouette score 0.547875
n_clusters = 6, silhouette score 0.524818
n_clusters = 7, silhouette score 0.523139
n_clusters = 8, silhouette score 0.486676
```

It looks like $k=5$ is our best choice. This makes sense, because we created our toy blob dataset to have five blobs. The silhouette score is highest when the K-means algorithm fits with five clusters chosen.

If your dataset is large, you can fit on only a small portion of the set when searching for the best value of k. This enables you to check more values of k by saving a lot of time per fit.

K-means++

As a reminder of the previous algorithm description, the first step of K-means is to randomly select cluster centers:

1. Pick the k initial cluster centers at random from points in the input data
2. Assign all the data paints to the cluster which they are closest
3. Move the k centroids to center of all the points inside the newly created clusters
4. Repeat until k clusters stop changing (for example, convergence)

The "at random" part of the step can cause long fit times, especially on large datasets. In addition, the K-means algorithm is **not fully deterministic** and somewhat prone to converge to local minima instead of the desired global minimum. These two shortcomings of the random initialization strategy have motivated the development of the **K-means++** method, which employs a smarter way to select the initial cluster centers. Aside from the smarter initialization strategy, the rest of the fit steps are the same. The K-means++ strategy forces large separation in the initial cluster centers working on the assumption that clusters are likely to be far from each other (while points within a cluster are close to each other). Scikit-learn makes it easy to use K-means++ by making it an arg in the base `KMeans` object introduced in the previous sections. Simply pass `init = 'k-means++'` and execute as demonstrated in the following code:

```
# instantiate k-means object with k-means++ init method
clus = KMeans(n_clusters=5, init='k-means++',
              tol=0.004, max_iter=300)
```

Mini batch K-means

The base K-means method visits all of the data points in each and every fit iteration, so large datasets can use large amounts of computer resources and time to fit. A method for circumventing this issue is to fit on **small batches chosen randomly** and continue choosing a new mini batch for each iteration until convergence. This method can reduce fit time significantly, however it raises the likelihood of converging to a local minima, so it should be used with caution. The following code shows how to implement the batched version of K-means with Scikit-learn and the `batch_size` arg:

```
# import module and instantiate k-means mini batch object
from sklearn.cluster import MiniBatchKMeans
clus = MiniBatchKMeans(n_clusters=5, batch_size=50,
                       tol=0.004, max_iter=300)
```

Hierarchical clustering

The goal of **hierarchical clustering** is to merge similar clusters in a hierarchical fashion, so that the number of clusters used for assignment is dependent on what level of hierarchy best fits your problem statement. The plot of clusters connected in a hierarchical fashion is called a **dendrogram**. It consists of a distance metric on the y-axis and data point records on the x-axis. Since the groupings are done in a hierarchical connection graph, the number of clusters is chosen by simply moving up and down the distance (y) axis.

The dotted lines in the dendrogram demonstrate the different levels of hierarchy and the resulting number of clusters for each. The highest distance corresponds to one cluster, and the lowest corresponds to a cluster for every data point. Of course, these are both unhelpful choices of hierarchy, and the correct answer is found somewhere in between:

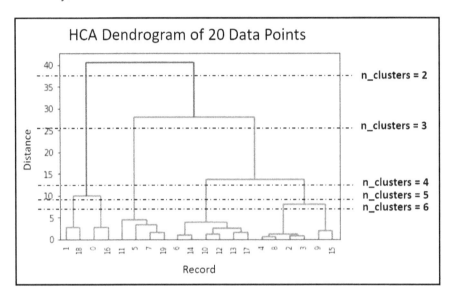

The first step in creating the dendrogram is to build what is usually called a **distance matrix**. The elements of the distance matrix are shown as follows:

$$
D = \begin{pmatrix}
l_{11} & l_{12} & \cdots & l_{1n} \\
l_{21} & l_{22} & \cdots & l_{2n} \\
\cdot & \cdot & \cdots & \cdot \\
\cdot & \cdot & \cdots & \cdot \\
\cdot & \cdot & \cdots & \cdot \\
l_{n1} & l_{n2} & \cdots & l_{nn}
\end{pmatrix}
$$

A more appropriate name however is **linkage matrix**, because the values that populate the cells of the matrix are a derived from of pairwise distance, called **linkage** (*l*). Linkage uses the conventional similarity metrics as its base. That is to say, you can use any of the Euclidean distance metrics introduced earlier in the chapter to find linkage. Linkage is a pairwise metric for comparing two candidate clusters for merger. This is the y-axis in the dendrogram plot, and lower values correspond to more similar clusters.

Remember, the goal of hierarchical clustering is to merge similar clusters in a hierarchical fashion. So, if you consider all available clusters as candidates for merging, the two with the lowest pairwise linkage will be chosen for merger. Popular derived linkage strategies are in the following list, with clusters [A] and [B] representing arbitrary clusters from the entire set of candidates:

- **Single linkage**: Smallest distance between any two points in clusters [A] and [B]
- **Complete linkage**: Largest distance between any two points in clusters [A] and [B]
- **Average linkage**: Average of the pairwise distances between all the points in clusters [A] and [B]
- **Ward's linkage**: Resulting gain in the SSE of all elements in the combined cluster [AB]

Sum squared error (**SSE**) is defined as the sum of the squared Euclidean distance from each point to the newly created centroid. So, this means that Ward's linkage scores each would-be cluster by how much spread/variance would exist among its members.

The **hierarchical clustering analysis** algorithm (**HCA**) can be written in two different ways. The first is in the agglomerative fashion, which starts with every data point being in its own cluster, then moving up and merging all the way to a single-cluster hierarchy. The second way is divisive in nature and starts with all data points assigned to a single huge cluster, then moves in the opposite direction. Agglomerative clustering is much more common in data mining.

What should you notice from the comparing cluster methods screenshot: Unlike means separation, hierarchical clustering did well to cluster all the different shapes of data. Of note is box B-1 of unstructured data, which consists of random points filling the whole space and having no discernible shape. It's instructive to study the behavior of each cluster algorithm on unstructured data so that you can build intuition on how the fit routine traverses data. Think of the unstructured case as a plot of the fit routine running wild. Since hierarchical clustering starts with a single cluster and then builds up (or the other way around), all data in B-1 is initially assigned to cluster one and then stays there, since there is never a compelling reason for the algorithm to move them. Scikit-learn employs a version of HCA that takes `n_cluster` as an input, so it forces a couple of points to be in cluster two and three, but otherwise they would have all stayed in cluster one during the entire fit routine.

Notable args for cluster object: you can use the `linkage` arg to pass linkage strategy, and then use the `affinity` arg to set the similarity metric used to derive linkage.

An example of applying HCA in Scikit-learn is included in the following code:

```
# generate blob example dataset
df = make_blobs()

# import module and instantiate HCA object
from sklearn.cluster import AgglomerativeClustering
clus = AgglomerativeClustering(n_clusters=5,
                           affinity='euclidean', linkage='ward')

# fit to input data
clus.fit(df)

# get cluster assignments
df['HCA Cluster Labels'] = clus.labels_

sns.lmplot(x='Feature_2', y='Feature_1',
           hue="HCA Cluster Labels", data=df, fit_reg=False)
```

You will see the following output on the execution of the preceding code:

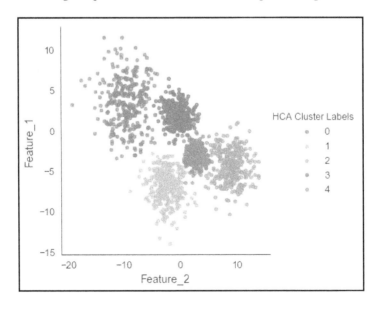

Reuse the dendrogram to find number of clusters

You only have to build the dendrogram once during an analysis. You can change the **level of hierarchy** used in the algorithm by simply moving the distance cutoff (the dotted line in our dendrogram) up and down. Since the level of hierarchy controls the **number of clusters**, you can use this to tune the quality of your clustering. The HCA algorithm scales notoriously badly as $O(n^3)$, which means that the time to fit rises as the cube of the number of input data points. This unfortunate time complexity is related solely to the construction of the dendrogram, so, when tuning for number of clusters, it is helpful to store the dendrogram for the next run. Reusing the dendrogram causes subsequent fits to be almost instantaneous. Like many other aspects of data mining, Scikit-learn has a built-in method to make this easy. You just need to pass the `memory = "dir_to_store"` and `compute_full_tree = True` arg so that no shortcuts are taken during the fit and the whole dendrogram is calculated and store in the directory of your choice. The following is an example code for reusing the dendrogram and fitting multiple times:

```
# find optimal number of clusters using silhouette score
# import metrics module
from sklearn import metrics

# generate blob example dataset
df = make_blobs()

# import module and instantiate HCA object
from sklearn.cluster import AgglomerativeClustering

# create list of k values to test and then use for loop
n_clusters = [2,3,4,5,6,7,8]
for num in n_clusters:
    HCA = AgglomerativeClustering(n_clusters=num,
                        affinity='euclidean', linkage='ward',
                        memory='./model_storage/dendrogram',
                        compute_full_tree=True)
    cluster_labels= HCA.fit_predict(df)
    S = metrics.silhouette_score(df, cluster_labels)
    print("n_clusters = {:d}, silhouette score {:1f}".format(num, S))
```

You will see the following output on execution of the preceding code:

```
n_clusters = 2, silhouette score 0.491869
n_clusters = 3, silhouette score 0.445017
n_clusters = 4, silhouette score 0.514050
n_clusters = 5, silhouette score 0.540089
n_clusters = 6, silhouette score 0.512037
n_clusters = 7, silhouette score 0.506730
n_clusters = 8, silhouette score 0.476728
```

It should be no surprise by this point that 5 is chosen as the best number of clusters.

Plot dendrogram

To recreate the dendrogram displayed in the chapter, you'll have to use the SciPy module, as Scikit-learn and Seaborn do not have a good solution for this routine as of yet. The following is the code you will need to make the plot:

```
# import scipy module
from scipy.cluster import hierarchy

# generate blob example dataset
df = make_blobs()

# Calculate the distance between each sample
Z = hierarchy.linkage(df, 'ward')

# Plot with Custom leaves (scroll down in console to see plot)
hierarchy.dendrogram(Z, leaf_rotation=90, leaf_font_size=8,
labels=df.index)
```

Density clustering

As opposed to defining similarity as solely a measure of distance between points, **density clustering** adds a correction for space covered by those points. You should know from grade school math class that density is given by the number of points per unit volume. After this correction, the number of points **in a given space** matters when defining clusters. As a consequence density clustering is very good at denoising, which means to exclude noisy outlier points when they lie outside the dense areas of the data. This clustering method also does not require you to know the number of clusters before you run the fit routine.

The most popular density clustering algorithm is called **DBSCAN**, and uses the cohesion concept to restrict the definition of density to include only data points within the cluster. You will often hear data mining professionals refer to this measurement as "local density of points". With Euclidean distance chosen as the similarity metric, you find density by dividing number points in the cluster by the **radius (ε)** of the cluster, or alternatively use a power (square or cube) of ε for better scaling.

The DBSCAN fitting routine starts with a couple inputs from you the practitioner. First, define a value for ε. Then, consider the space covered by ε as a neighborhood. Next, choose the minimum number of other points (`min_samples`) that you would expect to be in the same neighborhood in order to not be considered noise. The algorithm takes these inputs and assigns each point in the dataset one of the following labels:

- **Core point**: Has more than the `min_samples` points within its neighborhood
- **Border point**: Falls short of the `min_samples` requirement, but is itself in the neighborhood of a core point
- **Noise point**: Is not a core point or border point

Then, the algorithm finishes by combining core points that are within each others' neighborhood. These combined core points form the final clusters. Border points inside a cluster's neighborhood are assigned to that cluster. Noise points are not assigned to any cluster (and are given the value "-1" in Scikit-learn).

What should you notice from the comparing cluster methods screenshot: The method of means separation introduced earlier in the chapter defines similarity as the distance between points in a cluster, and grows/shrinks its clusters in a spherical manner during the fit process. As is demonstrated in box A-3 of the "Comparing Cluster Methods" screenshot, this can lead to spurious cluster assignments when the ground truth data has a non-spherical shape, or when points in one cluster are closer to points in another cluster than to their own cluster centroid. Density clustering performs better on this shape of data, as can be seen in box C-3. Also, notice how the algorithm fails to find the third cluster in C-5. This is because our chosen neighborhood size was too big and resulted in a merge of the two blobs. However, it did succeed in identifying noise, as can be seen by the black points surrounding the middle cluster. These black points are the ones Scikit-learn assigned the "-1" label. Lastly, study box C-1 to see what the DBSCAN algorithm does with unstructured data. There are no low density regions, so the algorithm finds one single cluster and assigns all points to that cluster.

Notable args for cluster object: Set `eps` with your value for ε, and use `min_samples` as described in the preceding algo description. You can choose the similarity metric using `metric`.

An example of applying DBSCAN in Scikit-learn is included in the following code:

```
# generate blob example dataset
df = make_blobs()

# import module and instantiate DBSCAN object
from sklearn.cluster import DBSCAN
clus = DBSCAN(eps=0.9, min_samples=5, metric='euclidean')
```

```
# fit to input data
clus.fit(df)

# get cluster assignments
df['DBSCAN Cluster Labels'] = clus.labels_

sns.lmplot(x='Feature_2', y='Feature_1',
           hue="DBSCAN Cluster Labels", data=df, fit_reg=False)
```

You will see the following output on the execution of the preceding code:

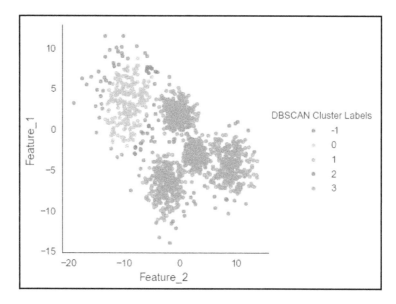

Notice how density clustering has a hard time finding clusters that are close to spherical and overlapping at the edges, demonstrating that it isn't the best method for clustering our toy blob dataset. Basic K-means would be a better choice. Even though DBSCAN failed to find all the clusters, it did do well to identify the noisy points. They are labeled "-1" in the preceding output plot. Keep this denoising ability in mind when you work on real-world problem statements, as it is often a desirable trait to have in a data mining method.

Spectral clustering

Spectral clustering builds a connection graph and groups points based on the connectivity of its constituent nodes. Unlike density clustering, you do have to know the number of clusters at fit time. The full details are beyond the scope of this book, but are summarized as follows:

A **similarity matrix** is built that compares the **affinity** of each data point to the rest of the points. Then, similar to the principal component analysis introduced in the previous chapter, eigenvectors are found, and the data is transformed into this new **affinity space**. Finally, a conventional clustering algorithm, such as *K-means*, is used to cluster the data in affinity space.

The similarity matrix is shown as follows, with elements of the table populated with pairwise affinity values (a_{ij}). A more helpful name for this particular similarity matrix is **affinity matrix**, but it's less popular nomenclature among data mining practitioners:

$$A = \begin{pmatrix} a_{11} & a_{12} & \cdots & a_{1n} \\ a_{21} & a_{22} & \cdots & a_{2n} \\ . & . & \cdots & . \\ . & . & \cdots & . \\ . & . & \cdots & . \\ a_{n1} & a_{n2} & \cdots & a_{nn} \end{pmatrix}$$

Any metric that returns a pairwise similarity score can be used to calculate affinity. I recommend using the nearest neighbors algorithm, because it brings a natural hyperparameter for you to tune, which is the number of neighbors (n_neighbors) to consider in the search.

At first blush, hierarchical clustering and spectral clustering seem to employ a similar method by defining a correlation matrix on the data. They are, however, quite different. Hierarchical clustering creates a linkage matrix populated by linkage distance and then clustered directly on these distances. Spectral clustering creates an affinity matrix populated with an affinity metric. Then, instead of clustering on the affinity metric, it transforms the matrix into lower-dimensional eigenvector space before clustering.

What you should notice from the "Comparing Cluster Methods" screenshot: Much like hierarchical clustering, spectral clustering did well to cluster all the different shapes of data. Of note is box D-1 of unstructured data. Since spectral clustering looks for connections between all data points and finished with a K-means clustering algorithm, the behavior on unstructured data is similar to means ceparation. This distinguishes it from the behavior of hierarchical clustering.

Notable args for cluster object: Set the affinity and the number of neighbors (if necessary) with the `affinity` and `n_neighbors` args. Then, choose the clustering algorithm with `assign_labels` and optionally pass the `n_init` arg to run the K-means algorithm more than once, and take the best fit.

An example of applying spectral clustering in Scikit-learn is included in the following code:

```
# generate blob example dataset
df = make_blobs()

# import module and instantiate spectral clustering object
from sklearn.cluster import SpectralClustering
clus = SpectralClustering(n_clusters=5, random_state=42,
                          assign_labels='kmeans', n_init=10,
                          affinity='nearest_neighbors', n_neighbors=10)

# fit to input data
clus.fit(df)

# get cluster assignments
df['Spectral Cluster Labels'] = clus.labels_

sns.lmplot(x='Feature_2', y='Feature_1',
           hue="Spectral Cluster Labels", data=df, fit_reg=False)
```

You will see the following output on the execution of the preceding code:

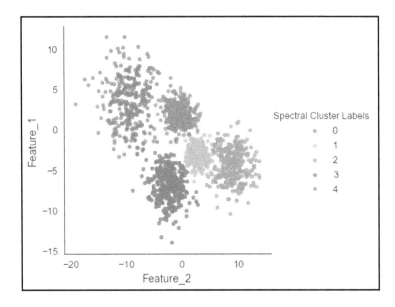

Summary

This chapter covered the background and thought process that goes into designing a clustering algorithm for data mining work. It then introduced common clustering methods in the field and illustrated a comparison between all of them with toy datasets. After reading this chapter, you should know the difference between algorithms that cluster based on means separation, density, and connectivity. You should also be able to see a plot of incoming data and have some intuition on whether clustering fits your mining project. In addition, you should have a good idea of what method to try first.

The next chapter will cover common prediction and classification strategies, as well as introducing the concepts of loss functions, gradient descent, and cross validation.

6
Prediction with Regression and Classification

This chapter will cover the basics of predictive modeling, covering topics related to the mathematical machinery, types of predictive models, and tuning strategies. For many readers, prediction is the ultimate goal of their work, so it is important to understand that this topic is a full field of its own. Take this chapter as an introduction and launching-off point for your learning.

The following topics will be covered in this chapter:

- Mathematical machinery, including loss functions and gradient descent
- Linear regression and penalties
- Logistic regression
- Tree-based classification, including random forests
- Support vector machines
- Tuning methodologies including cross-validation and hyperparameter selection

Scikit-learn Estimator API

One of the reasons **scikit-learn** is so popular is its ease of use. There are only a few, well thought-out API designs in the library and they are applied in a sweeping manner across many different methods and routines. This chapter will make use of the **Estimator API**. It's extremely straightforward, and, once you understand how to use it, you can try our new regression and classification estimator methods with ease, because they all work in the same way (in other words, they all make use of the Estimator API).

The steps are given as follows:

1. Import the module
2. Instantiate the estimator object (regression or classification model in the following diagram)
3. Fit the model-to-map input training data (X_train in the following diagram) to the ground truth y_train labels
4. Predict y_pred on the new test data (X_test in the following diagram)

It can also be represented as a **workflow diagram**:

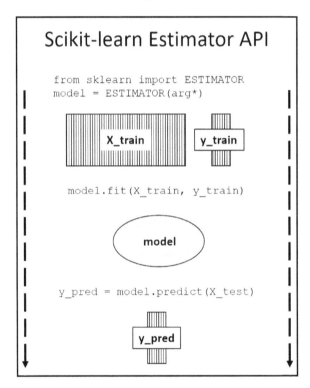

Introducing prediction concepts

Predicting the output value (that is, **regression**) or label (that is, **classification**) on future unseen data is a common final step in data mining projects.

Before reading the rest of this chapter, please be sure to digest the prerequisite concepts introduced in the *Basic data terminology* and *Basic summary statistics* sections in `Chapter 2`, *Basic Terminology and Our End-to-End Example*. In particular, the content on data types, variable types, and prediction metrics will be assumed as having been pre-learned throughout the entirety of the chapter.

The main strategy is to collect a training set and build a mapping function (that is, fit a **model**) from the input variables (X) to the output variable (y). Let's collect our assumptions before moving on:

- (**Assumption**) There is a relationship between X and y, namely that X are independent variables and y is dependent on X
- (**Assumption**) Future data will have the same distribution as the training set

If both assumptions hold, then you can build the model on a training set and apply the model to new unseen data to generate a meaningful prediction.

Mapping functions can model both linear and non-linear relationships and typically have multiple internal parameters that must be optimized for the best fit. Of course, we do not want to jump in and manually choose parameters of the mapping function, so we need to design an algorithm for building the function and finding the best parameters, which will allow our computing machines to learn the mapping function. If we can use mathematics to quantitatively describe what we want to get done, then our computers can do it for us. This means we have to quantitatively define the following:

- What **behavior** is important to our problem statement
- A **strategy** for optimizing that behavior

The most common strategy is to formulate the prediction algorithm as a minimization problem. In this mindset, we define **bad behavior** and how to minimize it. Bad behavior is defined as missed predictions and is quantified by a useful metric that measures the amount and extent of the misses, called **loss**. The function to calculate loss is appropriately named a **loss function** and typically compares the predicted output (y_{pred}) to the ground truth output variable (y). Loss can be minimized in a multitude of ways, but the most common is called **gradient descent** and uses a trick from differential calculus to move a system in the direction of minimization. The details of loss and gradient descent are presented in the following sections.

Furthermore, a number of model parameters for each prediction algorithm can be preset to affect the minimization path. These are called **hyperparameters** and are set independently of the minimization problem. The process of building and **tuning** a prediction model's hyperparameters to ensure its reliable generalization to new data is accomplished by following an established and systematic series of steps. This process will be described in the *Tuning a prediction model* section later in the chapter.

Prediction nomenclature

This chapter will use the *X, Y* terminology introduced in the *Variable types* section in `Chapter 2`, *Basic Terminology and our End-to-End Example,* with a couple of additions for describing the size of *X*. Here is a summary of the nomenclature used in the rest of the chapter:

- **X**: matrix of independent input variables
- x_i: i^{th} single record/row from *X*
- **Y**: matrix of ground truth dependent target variables
- y_i: i^{th} single record/row from Y
- y_{pred}: predicted target variable
- **m**: number of records in X
- **n**: number of features in X

The following is an example of the nomenclature applied to our `long_jump` dataset:

Size of X m = 6 n = 4		X			Y
Person	**Age**	**Height**	**Weight**	**Training Hours/week**	**Long Jump**
Thomas	12	57.5	73.4	6.5	19.2
Charlize	13	65.5	85.3	8.9	25.1
Vaughn	17	71.9	125.9	1.1	14.3
Vera	14	65.3	100.5	7.9	18.3
Vincent	18	70.1	110.7	10.5	21.1
Lei-Ann	12	52.3	70.4	0.5	10.6

Mathematical machinery

As mentioned previously, two pieces of mathematical machinery are essential for getting your computer to do the tedious job of model fitting. The first is an expression to quantify prediction error called the **loss function** and the second is a routine to minimize the prediction error by moving the parameters inside the algorithm toward the direction of lower loss, known as **gradient descent**.

Loss function

The **loss function** is the mathematical expression that calculates the loss of the model prediction. Remember that loss is a metric that quantifies bad behavior, or missed predictions. Each prediction method uses a different type of mapping (called the **hypothesis function**) so the loss function is tailored to each particular hypothesis type. For instance, linear regression hypothesizes that X can be mapped to y by a linear function (that is, by a straight line). So, a useful loss function in linear regression would calculate how far the prediction line is from each of the target y in the training set.

Let's start by taking a look at the linear regression hypothesis function. It applies linear mapping from input x to predicted target output y_{pred}, where x is one row from the matrix X, h is the hypothesis function, and θ variables are the slope and intercept values of the prediction/hypothesis line:

$$y_{pred} = h_\theta\left(x\right) = \theta_1 x + \theta_0$$

Now, we will move on to defining loss with the help of the toy data plotted in the following graph. If y are the the ground truth values and the hypothesis function, h_θ, provides the predictions that make up y_{pred}, then the following plot arises:

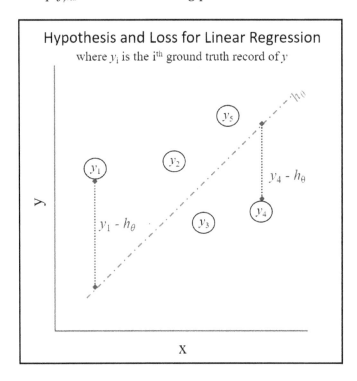

If we let the the blue (vertical dotted) lines in the plot ($y_i - h_\theta$) quantify bad behavior, then the sum of all of them becomes the loss in our system. So let's write that simple concept out mathematically and call the loss function J:

$$J(\theta) \propto \sum_{i=1}^{m} \left(y_{pred,i} - y_i\right)^2 = \mathbb{C} \sum_{i=1}^{m} \left(h_\theta\left(x_i\right) - y_i\right)^2$$

Total loss J is simply the sum of all the blue lines squared multiplied by a constant C. We square it so that the value of the blue line is always positive, causing us to score overshooting and undershooting predictions the same amount of bad. That's it! Now we have a useful loss function to quantify bad behavior, and we can move on to minimizing the bad behavior. Note that in the equation for $J(\theta)$, we've collapsed θ_1 and θ_2 into in the single variable θ for simplicity.

Many practitioners would call this a **cost function** instead of loss function. There are slightly different definitions for these two terms, but in practice they are used interchangeably. Be prepared to hear both terms in your day-to-day work.

Gradient descent

The next step is to have the computer learn parameters (θ) of the hypothesis function h_θ that minimizes the bad behavior (that is, missed predictions). Luckily, Sir Isaac Newton has our back and has given us a functioning piece of mathematical machinery to get the job done. The machinery is called **the derivative**, and is the basis for all differential calculus. However, we don't need the whole field of differential equations, just the one simple derivative.

Before we apply the derivative machinery, let's take a step back and remember what we are trying to accomplish. We want to minimize bad behavior. For that, we have a loss function that we are trying to minimize:

$$J\left(\theta\right) \propto \sum_{i=1}^{m} \left(y_{pred,i} - y_i\right)^2 = \mathbb{C} \sum_{i=1}^{m} \left(h_\theta\left(x_i\right) - y_i\right)^2$$

We will begin by visualizing the function of J(θ) in the following plot and annotating its prediction behavior:

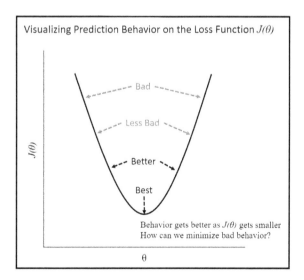

Notice how the function is convex like a bowl. This was, indeed, done on purpose and is part of the design of any good loss function. The convex shape gives us the ability to define a mathematical goal for our machinery. Minimizing bad behavior is now an exercise in traversing the loss function **J(θ)** towards the bottom of the bowl. So, if we land on the right side of the bowl, we want to move left across the function, which takes us towards the bottom. If we land on the left side, we want to do the opposite.

Our goal is becoming clearer and clearer, so now we can bring in the derivative. The derivative will direct our descent to the bottom of the bowl in a process called **derivative descent**. This concept is not nearly as scary as it sounds. In fact we can reason through the machinery by visualizing the goal and observing how we can reach it, all without any complicated equations. Remember our goal is to reach the bottom of the loss function J(θ) bowl. Start with the following diagram by looking at the plot on the left to visualize our goal, then read the observations in the table on right from top to bottom:

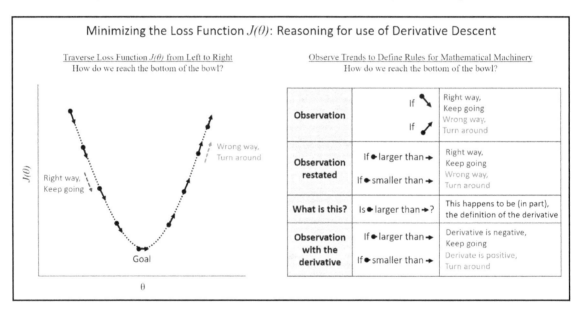

Hopefully, you now see the beauty of the derivative and why it's such a strong foundation for so many mathematical formulations. To summarize our example, derivative descent says the following:

- If the derivative is negative, keep going to the right by making $θ$ larger
- If the derivative is positive, turn around and go back to the left by making $θ$ smaller

The derivative is often described as the rate of change of one variable with respect to another. This translates in our example to the rate of change of *J* with respect to *θ*. The full definition of the derivative measures the direction (positive/negative) and the magnitude (large/small) of the change. To help build your intuition on derivative values a bit more, study the following graphs in order to visualize derivative values:

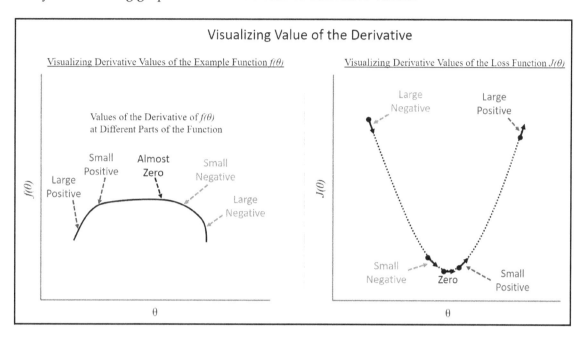

Because the derivative has both a magnitude and a direction, we can automate not only the descent direction, but also the size of each step. Large derivative values mean that we are in a steeper portion of the bowl curve, which indicates that we are far away from the bottom of the bowl. Small values mean that we are getting closer to the bottom. A zero value of the derivative means we've reached the bottom.

Make sure that you can map the magnitude and sign of the derivative onto our loss function before moving on to the rest of the section. You can go back and study the right side of the previous diagram if you are having trouble with the concept.

We are ready for the final step in the derivative descent routine. Larger values of the derivative mean that we are farther away, so we should take large steps toward the bottom. As we get closer to the bottom, the derivative drops, meaning that we should take smaller steps to avoid overshooting the bottom of the bowl. We achieve movement along the loss function by updating the value of θ. Recall that θ is a parameter of our hypothesis function. So, in linear regression, θ can be the intercept or the slope of the line to which we are trying to fit the data. Let's look again at the hypothesis function so that we are clear on what the θ values represent:

$$y_{pred} = h_\theta\left(x\right) = \theta_1 x + \theta_0$$

Notice that there are two parameters in our hypothesis function (θ_1 and θ_2), so full formulation of the loss function would produce two of the bowl plots, one for each parameter. Finally, we are ready to write the mathematical instruction to update the θ parameters with derivative descent. The strategy is to simply subtract the step size from the initial value of θ. The following equation shows the parameter update:

$$\theta_{updated} = \theta_{initial} - step\ size$$

Since the derivative tells us where we are on the function path, the step size should scale with the derivative. Remember, however, that we don't want to steps that are too large due to the possibility of overshooting the bottom of the bowl. We can control how the step size scales with the derivative by multiplying it by a scaling factor. This scaling factor is called the **learning rate**. If we substitute learning rate (α) and the derivative ($dJ/d\theta$) for step size, the derivative descent update equation looks like this:

$$\theta_{updated} = \theta_{initial} - \alpha \left(\frac{\mathrm{d}J\left(\theta\right)}{\mathrm{d}\theta}\right)$$

The analyst defines the learning rate to fit the problem statement. The considerations for the choice of learning rate are as follows:

- **Too large** learning rates will overshoot the bottom of the bowl and waste time bouncing back and forth.
- **Too small** learning rates will take a longer time to traverse the loss function as the update steps would be too small and would also waste time.

This section is titled **gradient descent**, but you may have noticed it only covered derivative descent. Don't be alarmed, because **gradient** is simply the term for a collection of derivatives, stored as a vector in a matrix, which is similar to our prediction nomenclature of using x to denote a single row of data, and X to denote a matrix consisting of multiple rows. The derivative is a single parameter's rate of change, while the gradient is multiple parameters' rate of change stored in a matrix.

Our linear regression loss function has multiple parameters (θ_1 and θ_2), so optimizing them is called gradient descent. If we only had one parameter, the process would be called derivative descent.

Fit quality regimes

Part of the model tuning process is to measure not only prediction accuracy on the training dataset, but also to measure it on a held-out test set. The test set, by definition, was not used in the model training. The purpose of checking against a test set is to test the generalizability of the model to new, unforeseen data. Fitting an overly complex mapping function to your training set may provide a high-prediction (that is, low-loss) score on the train set, but will likely fail on new data. This regime of quality is called **high variance** and means the model is overfitted to the training data. The opposite situation occurs if the mapping function is not complex enough to capture the information in the system. In this case, the prediction score, even on the training set, will be low. This regime of quality is called **high bias** and means the model is underfitted to the training data. The best models for prediction are somewhere in between the over and underfitting regimes, meaning that tuning the model is of crucial importance. The different model quality regimes are depicted in the following diagram:

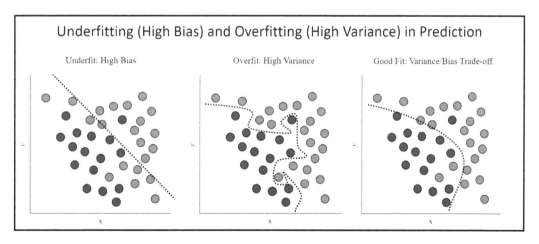

Finding the right trade-off between high bias and high variance is done by **tuning** a prediction model's hyperparameters to ensure its reliable generalization to new data. It is accomplished by following an established and systematic series of steps. This process will be described in the *Tuning a prediction model* section later in the chapter.

Regression

Regression models map input data to an output prediction of a numerical value, as opposed to classification models that predict categorical labels. The distinction is most easily conveyed through examples:

- Regression models can predict output such as housing prices, long jump distances, or number of home runs hit
- Classification models can assign labels such as true/false, low/medium/high risk, or which animal species

 I will use the prediction nomenclature described earlier in the chapter for the entire regression section. Make sure that you are familiar with the nomenclature before reading further.

Metrics of regression model prediction

When it comes to regression, a scoring system is needed to quantify the average error of the model. The metric for quantifying average error is appropriately called the **mean squared error** (**MSE**), and it's given by the following equation:

$$MSE = \frac{1}{m} \sum_{i=0}^{m} (y_{pred,i} - y_i)^2$$

The MSE score metric should look familiar to you, as it is the same form of the linear regression loss function. So, in this case, the score is essentially reporting the final loss of the model after minimizing the loss function. The downside of MSE is that it is affected by scale, so a good or bad score can only be defined for the specific input dataset according to its scaling. Datasets with larger input values will have larger MSE scores, and vice versa. This downside is usually not a hindrance for a single problem statement, but it makes case-to-case comparison impossible.

I recommend using a score that normalizes the MSE, so that you can compare scores between problem statements during your career, and build intuition over time. By this, I mean that a score of 0.8 on predicting housing prices means a similar quality as a score of 0.8 predicting long jump distances. The most popular normalized version of MSE is called the **coefficient of determination**, or by its often used nickname of **R^2 score**. If σ^2 is the **variance** of the dataset, the R^2 score is given by the following equation:

$$R^2 \; Score = 1 - \left(\frac{MSE}{\sigma^2} \right)$$

It is important to note that the best possible R^2 score is one.

Regression example dataset

We will use the `boston` dataset for our regression examples. You can use this helpful `get_boston()` function to create training and test sets for your work:

```
# import modules
from sklearn.datasets import load_boston
from sklearn.model_selection import train_test_split

# function to get boston dataset with training and test sets
def get_boston():
    # load the boston dataset
    dataset = load_boston()
    df = pd.DataFrame(dataset.data, columns=dataset.feature_names)
    df['MEDV'] = dataset.target
    df.index.name = 'record'
    # split into training and test sets
    X_train, X_test, y_train, y_test = \
        train_test_split(df.loc[:, df.columns != 'MEDV'],
                         df['MEDV'], test_size=.33, random_state=42)

    return [X_train, X_test, y_train, y_test]
```

Linear regression

The **linear regression** algorithm begins with the hypothesis that the data can be fit well to a straight line. The details of the model fit are used as the example in the *Loss function* and *Gradient descent* sections, so there is no need to repeat them here. Let's recall the equation for the hypothesis function *h* where θ variables are the slope and intercept values of the prediction/hypothesis line:

$$y_{pred} = h_\theta (x) = \theta_1 x + \theta_0$$

Now, we will look at the loss function:

$$J (\theta) \propto \sum_{i=1}^{m} (y_{pred,i} - y_i)^2$$

We can remove the "proportional to" (∝) relation and define the loss function explicitly by adding a constant *C*:

$$J (\theta) = \mathbb{C} \sum_{i=1}^{m} (h_\theta (x_i) - y_i)^2 = \frac{1}{2m} \sum_{i=1}^{m} (h_\theta (x_i) - y_i)^2$$

The constant *C* is only inserted to make the derivative easier to calculate during gradient descent, and its value is (1/2m).

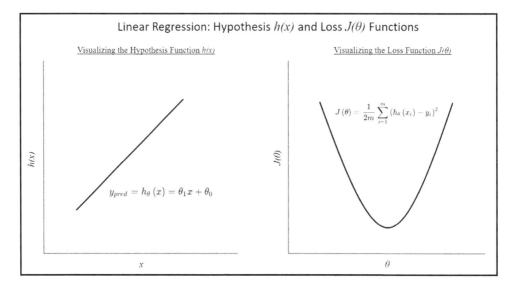

Linear regression with scikit-learn is done with the `LinearRegression` module:

```
### Linear Regression ###
# import modules
from sklearn.linear_model import LinearRegression
from sklearn.metrics import r2_score

# get moon dataset
X_train, X_test, y_train, y_test = get_boston()

#instantiate regression object and fit to training data
clf = LinearRegression()
clf.fit(X_train, y_train)

# predict on test set and score the predictions against y_test
y_pred = clf.predict(X_test)
r2 = r2_score(y_test, y_pred)
print('r2 score is = ' + str(r2))
```

You will see the following output on the execution of the preceding code:

```
r2 score is = 0.726
```

Extension to multivariate form

Most datasets will have more than one input feature, meaning that multivariate regression is required. Extending the univariate linear regression equations to their multivariate form is simple if we store each variable in a matrix. Let's start with a recall to the univariate form of the linear regression hypothesis function:

$$y_{pred} = h_\theta(x) = \theta_1 x + \theta_0$$

Remember that x is a single feature column. To accommodate multiple features, we use the nomenclature X to represent a matrix of features and capital Θ for the parameter values.

We will use x_i^j to represent the ith record/row and jth feature column. We will use $\theta_{[0,1]}^j$ to represent each univariate set of [θ_0 and θ_1] for the jth feature column:

$$X = \begin{bmatrix} x_0^1 & x_0^2 & x_0^3 \\ x_1^1 & x_1^2 & x_1^3 \\ x_2^1 & x_2^2 & x_2^3 \end{bmatrix}, \quad \Theta = \begin{bmatrix} \theta_{[0,1]}^1 \\ \theta_{[0,1]}^2 \\ \theta_{[0,1]}^3 \end{bmatrix}$$

The multivariate form of the linear regression hypothesis function can be written with matrix algebra conventions by multiplying matrix X and vector Θ:

$$h_\theta(X) = X\Theta$$

The linear regression loss function can be expressed in a vectorized form as well, with the squared term written as a matrix multiplied by its transpose:

$$J(\Theta) = \frac{1}{2m}(X\Theta - Y)^T(X\Theta - Y)$$

 To understand this expression fully requires a background in matrix algebra and is beyond the scope of this book. However, a full understanding is not required to use Scikit-learn's methods.

Regularization with penalized regression

As described in the *Fit quality regimes* section, **overfitting** occurs when the mapping function is too **complex**. Fitting an overly complex mapping function to your training set may provide a high-prediction (or low-loss) score on the train set, but is likely to fail on new data. This regime of quality is called **high variance**. The act of rectifying overfitting by adding correction terms is called **regularization**. The most common strategy for regularization is introducing penalty terms.

Recall how the loss function was used to define bad behavior in the form of missed predictions. An obvious next step for regularization is to add a term to the loss function specifically designed to penalize high complexity. It is added in this simple form:

$$penalized\ loss = loss\ function + penalty\ term$$

The multivariate linear regression loss function can be rewritten with penalty as follows:

$$J(\Theta) = \frac{1}{2m}(X\Theta - Y)^T(X\Theta - Y) + penalty\ term$$

Regularization penalties

The penalty terms in regularization methods target the parameters θ of the model. The strategy is built on the assumption that no single parameter θ should fully dominate the fit, so, if one grows too large, we should penalize the model and force it to learn smaller parameters across the board. Alternatively, a penalty term can be devised that completely removes small values of θ from the fit, essentially filtering in only the important features.

Recall how, in the multivariate formulation, the Θ matrix consists of θ values for each jth feature column. Taking the sum of all the absolute values of θ's in n feature columns and adding it directly to the loss function is called the **L1** penalty:

$$L1 \; penalized \; loss = loss \; function + \lambda \sum_{j=1}^{n} |\theta_j|$$

The λ value is added solely to give us a straightforward way to control the amount of penalty.

Linear regression with the *L1* penalty is called **lasso** regression. The multivariate linear regression loss function can be rewritten in lasso form with the *L1* penalty as follows:

$$J(\Theta) = \frac{1}{2m} (X\Theta - Y)^T (X\Theta - Y) + \lambda \sum_{j=1}^{n} |\theta_j|$$

Adding the sum of all squared values of θ's to the loss function is called the L2 penalty:

$$L2 \; penalized \; loss = loss \; function + \lambda \sum_{j=1}^{n} \theta_j^2$$

Linear regression with the *L2* penalty is called **ridge** regression. Now, the multivariate linear regression loss function can be rewritten in ridge form with the *L2* penalty as follows:

$$J(\Theta) = \frac{1}{2m} (X\Theta - Y)^T (X\Theta - Y) + \lambda \sum_{j=1}^{n} \theta_j^2$$

The *L1* penalty removes all features with small θ from the fit completely, as demonstrated by the red horizontal red line at the low values of θ in the following plots. The *L2* penalty does not remove any terms, but it penalizes more heavily as the values of θ get larger, because it is scaling as θ^2:

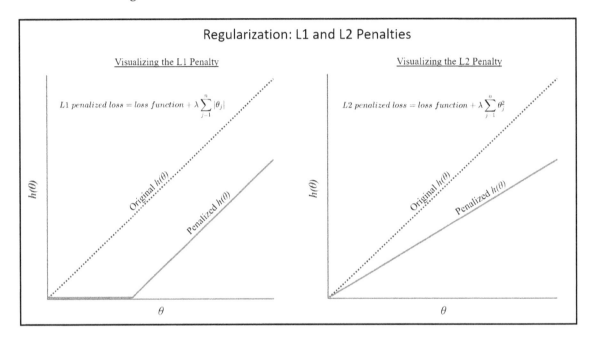

Scikit-learn makes adding *L1* and *L2* penalties easy with its **lasso** and **ridge** methods, respectfully. Let's look at lasso regression first, using the `alpha` arg to pass the λ value:

```
### Lasso Regression ###
# import modules
from sklearn.linear_model import Lasso
from sklearn.metrics import r2_score

# get moon dataset
X_train, X_test, y_train, y_test = get_boston()

#instantiate classifier object and fit to training data
clf = Lasso(alpha=0.3)
clf.fit(X_train, y_train)

# predict on test set and score the predictions against y_test
y_pred = clf.predict(X_test)
r2 = r2_score(y_test, y_pred)
print('r2 score is = ' + str(r2))
```

You will see the following output on the execution of the preceding code:

```
r2 score is = 0.705
```

Notice how the R^2 score is higher now that we've introduce some regularization into the linear regression model. Now, run the following code snippet to use ridge regression, again using the **alpha** arg to pass the λ value:

```
### Ridge Regression ###
# import modules
from sklearn.linear_model import Ridge
from sklearn.metrics import r2_score

# get moon dataset
X_train, X_test, y_train, y_test = get_boston()

#instantiate classifier object and fit to training data
clf = Ridge(alpha=0.3)
clf.fit(X_train, y_train)

# predict on test set and score the predictions against y_test
y_pred = clf.predict(X_test)
r2 = r2_score(y_test, y_pred)
print('r2 score is = ' + str(r2))
```

You will see the following output on the execution of the preceding code:

```
r2 score is = 0.724
```

The R^2 score rises even higher with ridge regression. Finding the right value of λ is part of hyperparameter tuning and is discussed in the *Grid search for hyperparameter tuning* section later in the chapter.

Classification

Classification models map input data to an output prediction of a categorical class label, as opposed to regression models that predict numerical values. The distinction is most easily conveyed through examples:

- Classification models can assign labels such as true/false, low/medium/high risk, or which animal species.
- Regression models can predict output such as housing prices, long jump distances, or number of home runs hit.

I will use the prediction nomenclature described earlier in the chapter for the entire classification section. Make sure that you are familiar with the nomenclature before reading further.

The rest of this chapter will cover some common methods used for prediction. The following is a group of plots comparing different prediction methods and how they map input data to target variables:

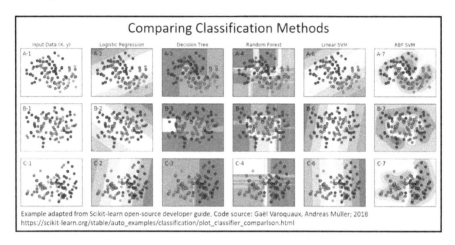

Classification example dataset

We will use a toy moon dataset for our classification examples. You can use this helpful `get_moon_data()` function to create training and test sets for your work:

```python
# import modules
from sklearn.model_selection import train_test_split
from sklearn.datasets import make_moons

# function to get toy moon set
def get_moon_data():
    # make blobs and split into train and test sets
    X, y = make_moons(n_samples=150, noise=0.4, random_state=42)
    X_train, X_test, y_train, y_test = \
        train_test_split(X, y, test_size=.33, random_state=42)
    return [X_train, X_test, y_train, y_test]
```

Metrics of classification model prediction

When it comes to classification, a scoring system is needed to quantify the predictive power of a model. Simple **accuracy** to measure the percentage of correct predictions is usually insufficient and can hide important model biases. For example, if you have unbalanced data with 90 examples of class A and only 10 examples of class B, a predictive model would score 90% on accuracy if it merely predicted everything as class A. Now, consider if class B is the label for cancer-stricken individuals in a medical study. This 90% accurate model is completely unacceptable and should be rejected. Alternative metrics have been designed to address these concerns. **Precision** focuses on positive examples and measures how well the model predicts positive points. **Recall**, on the other hand, adds consideration for false negatives and measures how well the model does at finding all the positive points. The industry standard for classification is the hybrid score that balances precision and recall by using the harmonic mean equation, known as F_1 **score**. See the following diagram for confusion matrix and metric scores information:

Confusion Matrix			Metric Scores

Confusion Matrix

Actual Class

		Positive	Negative
Prediction	Positive	True Positive	False Positive
	Negative	False Negative	True Negative

Metric Scores

$$Precision = \frac{True\ Positives}{True\ Positives + False\ Positives}$$

$$Recall = \frac{True\ Positives}{True\ Positives + False\ Negatives}$$

$$F_1\ Score = 2 * \frac{Precision * Recall}{Precision + Recall}$$

Multi-class classification

Multi-class classifiers have the ability to predict more than two target output labels. Binary classifiers are not inherently extendable to to multi-class problem. The two main strategies to extend them are the **one-versus-all** and **one-versus-one** classifications.

One-versus-all

The one-versus-all strategy builds a separate classifier for each label against all the other labels. Then, at prediction time it puts new data through all of the classifiers and assigns the data point the label with the highest score. This strategy builds one classifier for each label and puts all the data points through each classifier.

One-versus-one

The one-versus-one strategy builds a separate classifier for each pairwise combination of all the labels. Each classifier, therefore, only fits with data points in the current pair combination. At prediction time, the strategy puts new data through all of the classifiers and collects each output prediction as a single vote, then assigns the data point the label with the highest vote. This strategy builds more than one classifier for each label. If l is the number of labels, the number of small classifiers built by the one-versus-one strategy is given by the following formula:

$$number\ of\ classifiers = \frac{l(l-1)}{2}$$

The two strategies are summarized in the following table:

Input Labels 4 total	[A,B,C,D]
One-vs-rest Classifiers to be built = 4	[A] vs [B,C,D] [B] vs [A,C,D] [C] vs [A,B,D] [D] vs [A,B,C]
One-vs-one Classifiers to be built = 6	[A] vs [B] [A] vs [C] [A] vs [D] [B] vs [C] [B] vs [D] [C] vs [D]

Logistic regression

Despite the term regression being in the name, **logistic regression** is a binary classification technique. The hypothesis function is in the form of a sigmoid. If z is the linear combination of θ's and x's, then the hypothesis function for logistic regression is given by the following formula:

$$y_{pred} = h_\theta(z) = sigmoid(z)$$

The sigmoid function expanded is as follows:

$$sigmoid(z) = \frac{1}{1 + e^{-z}} \ , \ where \ z = \Theta^T X$$

Sigmoid functions are known for their S shape, which is precisely the reason that they are good for binary classification. The following graph shows the prediction strategy using the sigmoid functions. Values of z are collapsed onto either the top or bottom of the S shape. Values on the top are predicted as *1* and those on bottom are predicted as *0*:

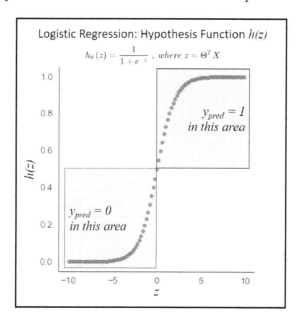

The loss function is a step function, meaning that it has more than one regime and has a different form for each of them. Before we get into the stepped nature, let's look at the general form and insert a placeholder `loss()` function call:

$$J\left(\theta\right) = loss(x_i, y_i)$$

The two different regimes are defined by the ground truth of the y_i label for that given x_i record. If y=1, then we are in one regime, if y=0, then we are in the other one. This behavior is represented by what's called a **step function**. The step function for logistic regression loss is as follows:

$$loss(x_i, y_i) = \begin{cases} -log(h_\theta) & if \ \ y = 1 \\ -log(1 - h_\theta) & if \ \ y = 0 \end{cases}$$

Visualizations of the loss function is are in the following diagram. Notice how, if the ground truth y=0, then the loss function blows up if the prediction approaches 1, and, of course the opposite is true if y=1:

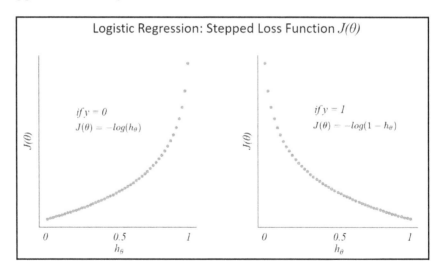

Logistic regression with Scikit-learn is done with the `LogisticRegression` module:

```
### Logistic Regression Classification ###
# import modules
from sklearn.linear_model import LogisticRegression
from sklearn.metrics import f1_score

# get moon dataset
```

```
X_train, X_test, y_train, y_test = get_moon_data()

#instantiate classifier object and fit to training data
clf = LogisticRegression(solver='lbfgs')
clf.fit(X_train, y_train)

# predict on test set and score the predictions against y_test
y_pred = clf.predict(X_test)
f1 = f1_score(y_test, y_pred)
print('f1 score is = ' + str(f1))
```

You will see the following output on the execution of the preceding code:

f1 score is = 0.749

You can plot the confusion matrix with the following code block:

```
### plot confusion matrix ###
from sklearn.metrics import confusion_matrix
import matplotlib.pyplot as plt
from matplotlib.colors import ListedColormap

# Creates a confusion matrix
cm = confusion_matrix(y_pred, y_test)

# create df and add class names
labels = ['top crescent', 'bottom cresent']
df_cm = pd.DataFrame(cm,
                     index = labels,
                     columns = labels)

# plot figure
plt.figure(figsize=(5.5,4))
sns.heatmap(df_cm, cmap="GnBu", annot=True)

#add titles and labels for the axes
plt.title('Logistic Regression \nF1 Score:{0:.3f}'.format(f1_score(y_test,
y_pred)))
plt.ylabel('Prediction')
plt.xlabel('Actual Class')
plt.show()
```

You will see the following output on the execution of the preceding code:

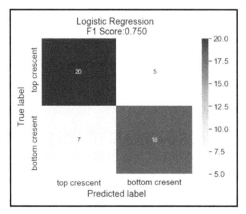

Regularized logistic regression

Note that the $L1$ and $L2$ penalties can be added to the end of the logistic regression loss function to fight overfitting. For details, see the precious section, entitled *Regularization penalties*. This type of penalty can be passed with the **penalty** arg, and the regularization constant is passed with the **C** arg. C is the inverse of λ, meaning that smaller values of C impart stronger penalty correction.

```
### Regularized Logistic Regression ###
clf = LogisticRegression(solver='lbfgs', penalty='l2', C=0.5)
```

Lastly, logistic regression can be turned into a multi-class classifier by using the **one-versus-rest** technique.

Support vector machines

The **support vector machine** (**SVM**) expands on the concepts behind the logistic regression model to create a classifier targeted directly at finding the maximum margin between classes. The edges of the margin are defined by the data points that are closest to the **decision boundary** separating the two predicted regions. These points are called the **support vectors**, and are, indeed, the source of the method's name. The following plots demonstrate the concepts of decision boundary, margin, and support vectors. Notice the difference in the decision boundaries between logistic regression and SVM:

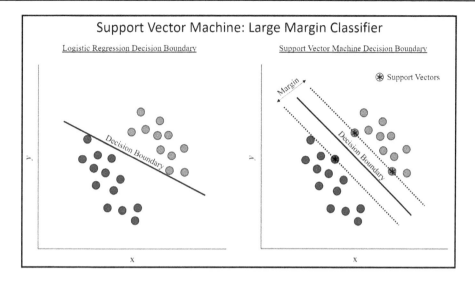

The corresponding boxes from the *Comparing Classification Methods* diagram demonstrate the rotation of the decision boundary imparted by the *SVM* fit:

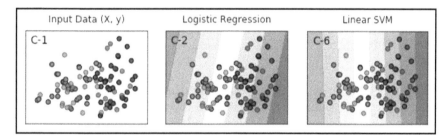

Recall that the logistic regression loss was calculated with a step function. The step function defined a different loss function for each prediction regime. In binary classification, these regimes are defined by the values of the ground truth labels. We have one regime for *y=1* and another regime for *y=0*. Let's start our SVM description by formulating the skeleton of a step function with placeholders for loss functions:

$$loss(x_i, y_i) = \begin{cases} loss_{y=1}(x_i, y_i) & if \ y = 1 \\ loss_{y=0}(x_i, y_i) & if \ y = 0 \end{cases}$$

Now, we will try to combine this relation into a single expression, while conserving the regime-based behavior defined by the step function. The first step is to add them together and use a proportional sign until we can explicitly define the final expression. The unfinished expression is as follows:

$$J\left(\theta\right) \propto loss_{y=1}\left(x_i, y_i\right) + loss_{y=0}\left(x_i, y_i\right)$$

Remember, our goal is to conserve the step function behavior. Let's focus on the y=1 regime first. If y=1, then we want only the $loss_{y=1}$ portion of the expression active. So, we need a way to turn off the $loss_{y=0}$ portion. The clever math trick for achieving this behavior is to multiple the $loss_{y=0}$ portion by *(1-y)*. Since *y=1*, and *1-y=0*, the $loss_{y=0}$ now equals zero and is turned off. The same trick is used by multiplying the $loss_{y=1}$ portion by *y*. Study this final expression for the *SVM* loss function to understand the trick:

$$J\left(\theta\right) = -\left(y_i\right)loss_{y=1}\left(x_i, y_i\right) - \left(1 - y_i\right)loss_{y=0}\left(x_i, y_i\right)$$

The obvious next question is: "What's the form of $loss(x_i, y_i)$?" The answer is a handy function called **hinge loss**. Hinge has a linear shape in the ON region, and flatlines at zero in the OFF region. Since the goal of model fitting is to minimize the loss function, the flatlined zero region will be the location of lowest loss. We will use this consequence of hinge shape to our advantage and position the hinge curve so that the flatlining occurs where we desire.

Recall that SVM is a classifier targeted directly at finding the maximum margin between classes. Instead of targeting a shared boundary (for example at zero) between y=1 and y=0 prediction regimes, we will separate into two boundaries and push each of them far from zero. We accomplish this task by positioning the hinge curves so that z values much greater than zero are preferred (or much less than zero on the negative side). This strategy is described in the following plots:

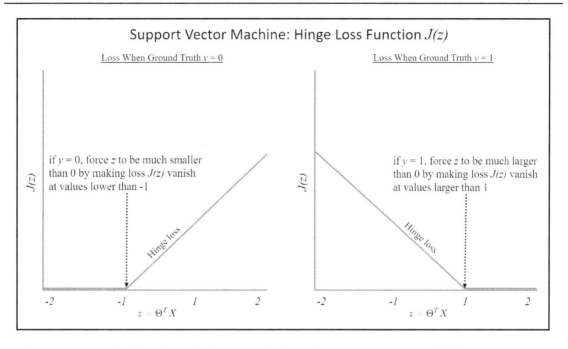

And we can now look back at the first graph from this section, with z added:

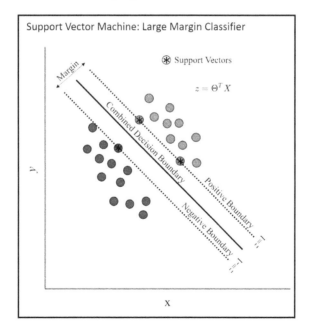

Soft-margin with C

Of course, not every dataset is cleanly separable with a large margin. The solution is to **soften** the definition of the margin. Softening the margin will allow a few samples to be mis-classed or to land inside the margin in order to build a more robust vector machine. This regularization method is applied using the C penalty `arg` in Scikit-learn. Lower C corresponds to a softer margin.

SVM classification with Scikit-learn is done with the `svm.svc` module:

```
### Support Vector Machine Classification ###
# import modules
from sklearn.svm import SVC
from sklearn.metrics import f1_score

# get moon dataset
X_train, X_test, y_train, y_test = get_moon_data()

#instantiate classifier object and fit to training data
clf = SVC(kernel="linear", C=0.5)
clf.fit(X_train, y_train)

# predict on test set and score the predictions against y_test
y_pred = clf.predict(X_test)
f1 = f1_score(y_test, y_pred)
print('f1 score is = ' + str(f1))
```

You will see the following output on the execution of the preceding code:

```
f1 score is = 0.749
```

The kernel trick

A conventional SVM is a binary, linear classifier. Interestingly, it can be extended to non-linear classifications with the use of the **kernel trick**. The kernel trick utilizes all the SVM machinery we've introduced and substitutes a new non-linear mapping function into the definition of the hypothesis function. The full mathematical formulation is beyond the scope of this book, but you should know that the kernel trick exists and how to apply it to an SVC. The most common kernel choice is a Gaussian kernel (using the radial basis function). Notably, it is the default kernel in Scikit-learn's classifier, so there is no need to pass any arg to use it.

However, there is a coefficient passed by the arg **gamma** that needs to be tuned for good classification. Gamma controls the width of the Gaussian mapping function that in turn controls the sphere of influence that each point has on the margin definition. Small values of gamma mean a large radius and less non-linearity. In fact, the smaller you set gamma, the more the SVM performs like the linear kernel version. Read the *Tuning a prediction model* section for instructions on how to tune hyperparameters like this one:

```
### SVM with Gaussian Kernel Classification ###
# instantiate classifier object and fit to training data
clf = SVC(gamma=2, C=1)
clf.fit(X_train, y_train)

# predict on test set and score the predictions against y_test
y_pred = clf.predict(X_test)
f1 = f1_score(y_test, y_pred)
print('f1 score is = ' + str(f1))
```

Lastly, SVM can be turned into a multi-class classifier by using the one-versus-one technique.

Tree-based classification

Tree-based methods apply transparent decision logic in a sequential fashion to make a prediction. The nature of their straightforward decision making mimics a human logic flow. These methods inherently handle multi-class problems without any special strategy and can handle both numerical and categorical inputs. Categorical inputs do require encoding for the best results. The most common encoding strategy for tree classifiers is **one-hot encoding**, which was introduced in the *Handling categorical data* section of Chapter 4, *Cleaning and Readying Data for Analysis*.

The largest downside of single-tree learning with **decision trees** is that they tend to overfit because they grow too complex. This problem was corrected with a brilliant insight from Leo Breiman in 2001. He constricted the depth of the trees and the features in each one to make them learn a weak (or underfit) model. He then built many of these weak learner trees to create an ensemble and had them all vote on the prediction. The result was a model that tuned itself and was very generalizable to new unforeseen data.

Decision trees

The **decision tree** classifier will build a chain of logic very similar to how a human would make a decision. This results in a very transparent decision function that we can understand. The tree starts with all the data in a **source node**, then branches into two nodes using some feature in the data. For instance, in the following example tree, the first branch was built on the feature, *sunny afternoon?* The tree keeps branching until it reaches terminal nodes, called **leaf nodes**. Each level of nodes is a new **depth** value. After the tree is built, predictions on new data (*y_pred*) are done by traversing the tree from the source node to whichever leaf node the new example reaches. Study the following example diagram:

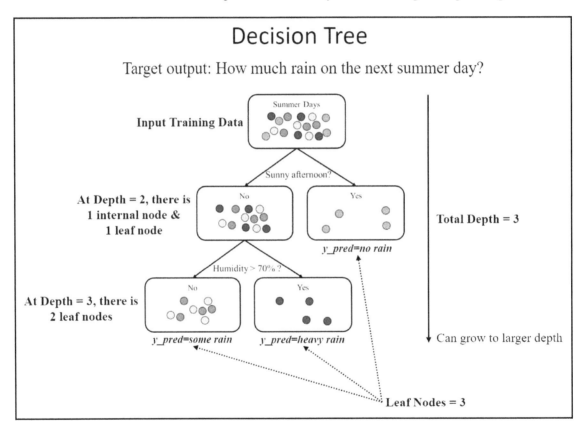

Node splitting with Gini

The decision tree algorithm must learn where and how to split into nodes on its own. It accomplishes this by a very simple relation based on **impurity**. Impurity is a measure of how reliable the prediction is for data points in the current node. Translated to mathematics, this is how well the node would classify a randomly selected data point within it based on the distribution of its current contents. The lowest possible impurity is 0, and occurs when all of the examples in a node are the same class. Of course, only perfect leaf nodes will have *impurity=0*. The decision on where to split comes from cycling through input features and their entire ranges to find which split location results in the lowest impurity in the child nodes. If *Imp* is impurity, the location to split is found by solving the following minimization problem:

$$location\ to\ split\ node = min(Imp_{child1} + Imp_{child2})$$

The following diagram shows the child nodes for which we want to minimize the sum of impurities:

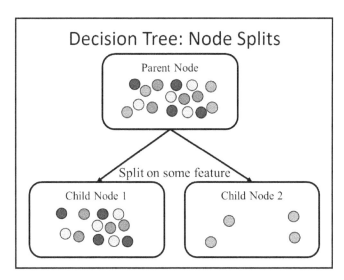

The next step is to quantify impurity. There are a few popular methods, but the outcome is the same in most cases, so you effectively only need to know one of them. Scikit-learn uses **Gini** as its default measurement of impurity on decision tree node splitting. If the list of i classes in the current node is [1, 2, 3,....., j] and the probability of picking the right class at random for an example data point in that node is p, then Gini is given by the following equation:

$$Gini\ imp = 1 - \sum_{i=1}^{j} p_i^2$$

Decision tree classification in Scikit-learn is done with the `DecisionTreeClassifier` module. You can constrict the depth of the trees with the `max_depth` arg:

```
### Decision Tree Classification ###
# import modules
from sklearn.tree import DecisionTreeClassifier
from sklearn.metrics import f1_score

# get moon dataset
X_train, X_test, y_train, y_test = get_moon_data()

#instantiate classifier object and fit to training data
clf = DecisionTreeClassifier(max_depth=4, random_state=42)
clf.fit(X_train, y_train)

# predict on test set and score the predictions against y_test
y_pred = clf.predict(X_test)
f1 = f1_score(y_test, y_pred)
print('f1 score is = ' + str(f1))
```

You will see the following output on the execution of the preceding code:

```
f1 score is = 0.739
```

Random forest

Random forest is an **ensemble** learning algorithm that is built with a series of constituent **weak leaner** trees, regularly extending into hundreds of learners. The constituents then vote to form the prediction. The result is a method that generalizes well and often requires little (or no) tuning by the practitioner. Please study the following diagram to see the full picture of the forest:

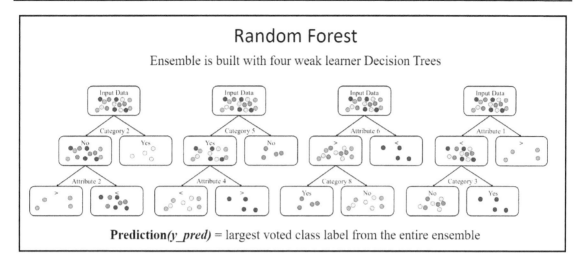

Avoid overfitting and speed up the fits

Random forest is very good at avoiding high-variance overfitting, due to the weak learners' inability to fit an overly complex mapping function. The decision trees are made weak by employing two main strategies:

- Constricting their depth so they can't overfit with a complicated decision function
- Holding data points and features out during fit so they lack enough information to overfit

The brilliance in these strategies is also exemplified by both resulting in a speedup of the fit. Smaller trees with less information to parse fit much faster than large complicated trees.

To decide which features (n) to make available for each node split, a good rule of thumb is simply to take the *sqrt(n)* features chosen at random.

Built-in validation with bagging

Another remarkable outcome of the weak learner strategy becomes apparent when we focus on the examples (or data points) chosen for each tree. Some are purposefully left out with a strategy called **bagging**, which randomly chooses a fraction of the sample to add to the bag, and the rest is left **out-of-bag** (**OOB**). The OOB set becomes an internal validation set. So, each tree that is built has an OOB set to predict against. Because of this outcome, you usually don't have to apply any further cross-validation strategies to test robustness of a random forest model.

Bagging is usually done "with replacement." This means that duplicates are allowed in each bag, and is called **bootstrapping**. The main consequence of the bootstrap in the classification context is to artificially add more variation between each bag.

Random forest classification in Scikit-learn is done with the RandomForrestClassifier module. You can choose the number of constituents with the n_estimators arg, set the available features in each node split with the max_features arg, and constrict the depth of the trees with the max_depth arg:

```
### Random Forest Classification ###
# import modules
from sklearn.ensemble import RandomForestClassifier
from sklearn.metrics import f1_score

# get moon dataset
X_train, X_test, y_train, y_test = get_moon_data()

#instantiate classifier object and fit to training data
clf = RandomForestClassifier(max_depth=4, n_estimators=4,
                             max_features='sqrt', random_state=42)
clf.fit(X_train, y_train)

# predict on test set and score the predictions against y_test
y_pred = clf.predict(X_test)
f1 = f1_score(y_test, y_pred)
print('f1 score is = ' + str(f1))
```

You will see the following output on the execution of the preceding code:

```
f1 score is = 0.775
```

You can tell the random forest model to calculate the OOB score for validation by passing the oob_score arg during object instantiation:

```
### Use OOB for Validation Set ###
# instantiate classifier object and fit to training data
clf = RandomForestClassifier(max_depth=4, n_estimators=10,
                             max_features='sqrt', random_state=42,
                             oob_score=True)
clf.fit(X_train, y_train)

# score the predictions with OOB
oob_score = clf.oob_score_
print('OOB score is = ' + str(oob_score))
```

You will see the following output on the execution of the preceding code:

```
OOB score is = 0.73
```

Tuning a prediction model

Tuning your prediction model is vital for getting the best possible output for your data mining work. There are two types of parameters introduced in this chapter. The first are **internal parameters** of the hypothesis function, and are stored as individual θ's in the weights vector Θ. These parameters are tuned during the minimization of the loss function. The second type are constants added to the loss function or the minimization (for example, gradient descent) function that influences the tuning of the internal parameters, and are called **hyperparameters**. The *hyperparameters* are the subject of the tuning strategies in this section.

 Hyperparameter tuning is often referred to as **tuning the knobs** by practitioners in the field. This is a call-back to the analog days of engineering, when analytical machines had actual physical knobs. Back then, the tuning strategy was usually of the trial-and-error type, or the more appropriately named "guess-and-check."

Cross-validation

In order to estimate the generalizability of future data, a careful partitioning of the input dataset is imperative and is the best chance you have at quantifying estimated performance on unforeseen data. Recall that high-variance overfits do not translate well when applied to new data. See the *Fit quality regimes* section earlier in the chapter for more details. As a practitioner, avoiding the high-variance regime should be at the forefront of your mind in any prediction work you do. The goal of **cross-validation** is to reliably estimate generalizability, so you can tune confidently based on the estimations. The first step is adding a **validation set** to the **training** (X_train) and **testing sets** (X_test) introduced earlier in the chapter.

Introduction of the validation set

It may be tempting to ask why we can't build a model on the **training set**, score it on the **testing set**, tune a knob, and then rinse and repeat. The reason this strategy is non-optimal is because the test set actually informs the next knob turn (or hyperparameter value). This means it no longer is a true test set as it is part of the training process. The correction comes with the introduction of a **validation set** that is split off from the training set. This allows the test set to sit unseen until the end of the training process, only to be used for actual quantitative scoring of generalization. The following diagram depicts the extra split to create the validation set:

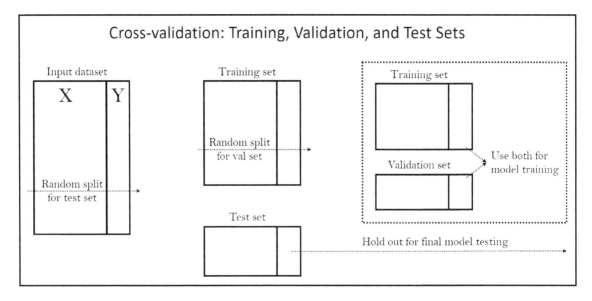

The usage of a validation set is easy with Scikit-learn, using the following test:

```
### Cross Validation ###
# load iris and create X and y
from sklearn.datasets import load_iris
dataset = load_iris()
X,y = dataset.data, dataset.target

# import module
from sklearn.model_selection import train_test_split

# create train and test sets
X_train, X_test, y_train, y_test = \
        train_test_split(X, y, test_size=.33)
```

```
# create validation set from training set
X_train, X_val, y_train, y_val = \
        train_test_split(X, y, test_size=.33)
```

Multiple validation sets with k-fold method

The most common strategy for cross-validation is the **k-fold method**, which involves slicing the data into multiple **folds** and then cycling through them make a train/val set combination for each fold. Then, if you are tuning knobs, you build a separate model on each fold and average the scores for each knob position. The following diagram demonstrates the strategy:

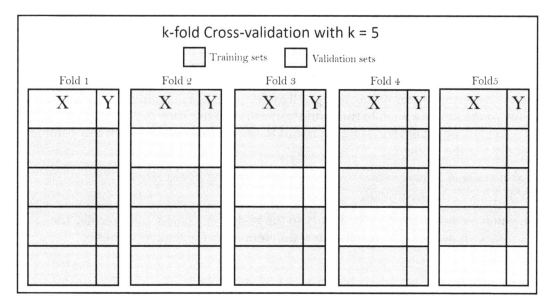

Scikit-learn has the `cross_val_score` module that can be used to fit a model with multiple folds and print the scores for each fold. The following is an example using logistic regression as a classifier and using the arg **cv=5** for five-fold cross validation:

```
### k-fold Cross Validation ###
# load iris and create X and y
from sklearn.datasets import load_iris
dataset = load_iris()
X,y = dataset.data, dataset.target

# import modules
from sklearn.linear_model import LogisticRegression
from sklearn.model_selection import cross_val_score
```

```
from sklearn import metrics
from sklearn.model_selection import train_test_split

# create train and test sets
X_train, X_test, y_train, y_test = \
        train_test_split(X, y, test_size=.33)

# instantiate classifier object and pass to cross_val_score function
clf = LogisticRegression(solver='lbfgs', multi_class='ovr')
scores = cross_val_score(clf, X_train, y_train, cv=5, scoring='f1_macro')
print(scores)
```

You will see the following output on the execution of the preceding code:

```
[0.9280303 0.92207792 0.88854489 0.95848596]
```

Grid search for hyperparameter tuning

The act of hyperparameter tuning is typically referred to as knob tuning. This is because it requires you to define a knob to turn and the position of the knob at you want to try. The GridSearchCV object is very straightforward to use for this task. You define a parameters dictionary like the following:

```
parameters = {'parameter1':['knob position 1', 'position2'],
'parameter1':['position1', 'position2]'}
```

Then, you pass the parameters dictionary to the grid search object and execute. The following example uses grid search to test different kernel types and values of C for a SVM classifier:

```
### Grid Search with k-fold Cross-validation ###
# load iris and create X and y
from sklearn.datasets import load_iris
dataset = load_iris()
X,y = dataset.data, dataset.target

# import modules
from sklearn.svm import SVC
from sklearn.model_selection import GridSearchCV
from sklearn import metrics
from sklearn.model_selection import train_test_split

# create train and test sets
X_train, X_test, y_train, y_test = \
        train_test_split(X, y, test_size=.33)
```

```
# instantiate svc and gridsearch object and fit
parameters = {'kernel':('linear', 'rbf'), 'C':[1, 5, 10]}
svc = SVC(gamma='auto')
clf = GridSearchCV(svc, parameters, cv=5, scoring='f1_macro')
clf.fit(X_train, y_train)

# print best scoring classifier
print('Best score is = ' + str(clf.best_score_))
print('Best parameters are = ' + str(clf.best_params_))
```

You will see the following output on the execution of the preceding code:

```
Best score is = 0.9702253302253303
Best parameters are = {'C': 5, 'kernel': 'rbf'}
```

Another in the long line of convenience methods from scikit learn is the ability to use the grid search object directly as a trained classifier on new data. This means the `clf` object in our grid search example is ready to be used as a prediction model right away:

```
# use the resulting classifier to predict on new data
y_pred = clf.predict(X_test)
```

Summary

This chapter covered the basics behind using a computer to learn prediction models by introducing the loss function and gradient descent. It then introduced the concepts of overfitting, underfitting, and the penalty approach to regularize your model during fits. It then covered common regression and classification techniques, and the regularized versions of each of these where appropriate. Large margin and tree-based classification were introduced in an intuition-driven manner. The chapter finished with a discussion of best practices for model tuning, including cross-validation and grid search. After reading this chapter, you should have a full picture of what the computer is doing when you ask it to learn a prediction model. You should now have intuition on what methods to try on your problem statement and how to tune and validate your models.

The next chapter will cover the advanced topic of deploying the transformation, clustering, and/or prediction models you've built, as well as the importance of thinking of a sequential chain of techniques as a single data mining pipeline.

7
Advanced Topics - Building a Data Processing Pipeline and Deploying It

This chapter will cover the strategy of building a data analysis pipeline and deploying it to run in production on future, incoming data. It will also cover persistent model storage, which is required to distribute for deployment. This chapter will then cover the specific consequences that Python's interpreted nature has on deployment.

The following topics will be covered in this chapter:

- Pipelining your analysis
- Storing a model for deployment
- Loading a deployed model
- Python-specific deployment concerns

Pipelining your analysis

A **pipelined** analysis is a series of steps stored as a single function or object. On top of providing a framework for your analysis, the most important reason for pipelining becomes apparent upon examining what is required to reproduce your workflow or apply it to new data. Now that you've seen a nice collection of various data mining methods, it's a good time to acknowledge some facts:

- Most analysis workflows have multiple steps (cleaning, scaling, transforming, clustering, and so on)
- In order to reproduce the workflow, all of the steps must be done in the exact right order

- Failure to reproduce the steps exactly can result in bad information, often failing silently
- Humans make mistakes, so we need to guard against those mistakes

The perfect tool for guarding against mistakes is to build a pipeline, test it locally, and deploy the entire pipeline as a finished product.

 It is a good idea to build your pipeline as you develop your analysis workflow. This will allow you to have confidence that the steps you applied are indeed captured correctly in the pipeline.

Scikit-learn's pipeline object

Scikit-learn has a full service `Pipeline` object that is compatible with objects that use both the transformer and estimator APIs. It can also take `GridSearchCV` as a step in the pipeline, so you can use the *pipeline* for tuning and the result will automatically be stored in the *pipe*.

For our first example, we will build a pipeline that transforms the data with `PCA` and then predicts labels with `LogisticRegression`. Let's start by loading the `iris` dataset and required modules, and splitting the data into a `train`/`test` set. We will use **k-fold cross-validation** in the grid search, so no need to make a separate validation set. Let's start with the following code:

```
### Building a Pipeline ###
# load iris and create X and y
from sklearn.datasets import load_iris
dataset = load_iris()
X,y = dataset.data, dataset.target

# import modules
from sklearn.decomposition import PCA
from sklearn.linear_model import LogisticRegression
from sklearn.pipeline import Pipeline
from sklearn.model_selection import GridSearchCV
from sklearn.model_selection import train_test_split

# create train and test sets
X_train, X_test, y_train, y_test = \
        train_test_split(X, y, test_size=.33)
```

We will first look at pseudocode for the use of the `Pipeline` object. The process begins by importing `transformer` and `estimator` modules and instantiating the object exactly how we've done in the previous chapters. Then, we create the `Pipeline` and pass the steps as a list, in the order we'd like them to execute. This list can grow larger than two steps. You can give each step a helpful name that will help you remember its purpose. Most practitioners simply use the name of the method here, such as `PCA`, `SVC`, or `Random Forest`. Finally, we can use the entire pipeline as any other method with the estimator API, with the `fit()` and `predict()` methods. Take a look at the following pseudocode version that outlines the steps:

```
### this is pseudocode. it will not execute ###
# import modules
from sklearn.pipeline import Pipeline
from sklearn import transformer
from sklearn import estimator

# instantiate the transformer and classifier objects
method1 = transformer(args)
method2 = estimator(args)

# instantiate a pipeline and add steps to the pipeline
pipe = Pipeline([('helpful name 1', method1), ('helpful name 2', method2)])

# print list of steps with names
print(pipe.steps[0])

# fit and predict
pipe.fit(X_train,y_train)
pip.predict(X_test)
```

Now, we can instantiate the `transformer` and `classifier` objects and feed them into the pipeline (named `pipe`):

```
# instantiate the transformer and classifier objects
pca = PCA()
logistic = LogisticRegression(solver='liblinear', multi_class='ovr', C=1.5)

# instantiate a pipeline and add steps to the pipeline
pipe = Pipeline(steps=[('pca', pca), ('logistic', logistic)])
```

Next, we will create the **parameter grid** that the grid search will use and instantiate the grid search object. Here, we will test a few values of n_components for PCA and C for **logistic regression** using **5-fold cross-validation**. Finally, we fit our model to the data and print out the best parameters:

```
# set the parameter grid to be passed to the grid search
param_grid = {
    'pca__n_components': [2, 3, 4],
    'logistic__C': [0.5, 1, 5, 10],
}

# instantiate the grid search object and pass the pipe and param_grid
model = GridSearchCV(pipe, param_grid, iid=False, cv=5,
                     return_train_score=False)

# fit entire pipeline using grid search and 5-fold cross validation
model.fit(X_train, y_train)
print("Best parameter (CV score=%0.3f):" % model.best_score_)
print(model.best_params_)
```

You will see the following output on the execution of the preceding code:

```
Best parameter (CV score=0.961):
{'logistic__C': 10, 'pca__n_components': 4}
```

The full pipeline model can be used to predict new data with the .predict() method:

```
# use the resulting pipeline to predict on new data
y_pred = model.predict(X_test)
```

Deploying the model

Often in a production environment, deployment is the step where you release your model into the wild and let it run on unforeseen data. However, data mining also produces many local analysis workflows; that don't necessarily need to deploy but do need to be stored and re-loaded later in order to reproduce the analysis. Both of these use cases require what is called **model persistence**. The term *persistence* means the model needs to be stored and loaded for later use. Python is an object-oriented language and appropriately scikit-learn uses objects for most of its analysis routines. Storing an object is not as simple as storing a basic text file full of strings. It instead requires a process called **serialization** to store in a reliable and error-free manner. One of the most popular serialization packages is a Python core library, pickle. It's what we will use for our serialization examples.

Serializing a model and storing with the pickle module

The `Pickle` module is compatible with Scikit-learn's `transformers` and `estimators`. Conveniently (and more importantly), it is also compatible with Scikit-learn's grid search and `pipeline` objects. It is very easy to use, as serialization and storage are accomplished with a single method called `.dump()`. The following example will use `pickle` to serialize our pipeline model and store it in a file named `model.pkl`:

```
### Store Model for Later with Pickle ###
# import module
import pickle

# save the pipeline model to disk
pickle.dump(model, open('./model_storage/model.pkl', 'wb'))
```

Loading a serialized model and predicting

When we are ready to use the model either in production or locally, we simply load back up with `pickle`, store it in a new local object. We can name the new loaded model object `model_load` and after loading and deserializing with the `.load()` method. Then, we can use `model_load` as if it were the original version of the model. See the following code example for a demonstration:

```
# load the pipeline model from disk and deserialize
model_load = pickle.load(open('./model_storage/model.pkl', 'rb'))

# use the loaded pipeline model to predict on new data
y_pred = model_load.predict(X_test)
```

Python-specific deployment concerns

Python is not a compiled language. It is interpreted at the time of execution. It is important to remember that, when you follow the steps in this chapter, you are not pickling an executable program. You are simply pickling an object. At load time, the environment must be compatible with the contents of the object. Often, that means matching versions, as libraries change over time. Also, the default serialization protocol for `pickle` is not compatible with Python 2, so you will have to change the protocol if switching Python versions.

Lastly, the pickled object is similar to a ZIP file in that anyone can bundle up anything inside it and you will not know it until you unpickle/unzip it. Security should always be a concern with any file types that are not transparent.

 You should read the main `pickle` doc page for descriptions of compatibility and security before using. It can be found here: `https://docs.python.org/3/library/pickle.html`.

Summary

This chapter covered a strategy for pipelining and deploying using built-in Scikit-learn methods. It also introduced the `pickle` module for model persistence and storage, as well as Python-specific concerns at deployment time. I encourage you to return to the code from `Chapter 2`, *Basic Terminology and Our End-to-End Example*, and build the entire end-to-end example data mining workflow as a Scikit-learn pipeline.

There's no substitute for practice, so grab some freely available data sets and solve as many real-world problems as you can find. Try your hand at a few analytics competitions and share your code with a friend for review and discussion. Identify the concepts that are toughest for you, and then hunt down explanations from other instructors or authors to get a different viewpoint on the topic. Don't let yourself off the hook until you fully understand the concepts.

The topics covered in this book are the foundations for modern machine learning and the burgeoning field of artificial intelligence. You cannot afford to have only a partial understanding of these concepts. Finally, take a look at the suggested reading from `Chapter 1`, *Data Mining and Getting Started with Python Tools*, if you'd like to dig further into the concepts introduced in this book.

Thank you for reading my book.

Other Books You May Enjoy

If you enjoyed this book, you may be interested in these other books by Packt:

Bayesian Analysis with Python - Second Edition
Osvaldo Martin

ISBN: 9781789341652

- Build probabilistic models using the Python library PyMC3
- Analyze probabilistic models with the help of ArviZ
- Acquire the skills required to sanity check models and modify them if necessary
- Understand the advantages and caveats of hierarchical models
- Find out how different models can be used to answer different data analysis questions
- Compare models and choose between alternative ones
- Discover how different models are unified from a probabilistic perspective
- Think probabilistically and benefit from the flexibility of the Bayesian framework

Big Data Analysis with Python
Ivan Marin

ISBN: 9781789955286

- Use Python to read and transform data into different formats
- Generate basic statistics and metrics using data on disk
- Work with computing tasks distributed over a cluster
- Convert data from various sources into storage or querying formats
- Prepare data for statistical analysis, visualization, and machine learning
- Present data in the form of effective visuals

Leave a review - let other readers know what you think

Please share your thoughts on this book with others by leaving a review on the site that you bought it from. If you purchased the book from Amazon, please leave us an honest review on this book's Amazon page. This is vital so that other potential readers can see and use your unbiased opinion to make purchasing decisions, we can understand what our customers think about our products, and our authors can see your feedback on the title that they have worked with Packt to create. It will only take a few minutes of your time, but is valuable to other potential customers, our authors, and Packt. Thank you!

Index

5

5-fold cross-validation 166

A

accuracy 141
affinity 117
affinity matrix 117
affinity space 117
alpha arg 139
Anaconda distribution
  installing 12
  installing, on Linux 12
  installing, on macOS 13
  installing, on Windows 13

B

backward direction 84
backward sequential selection 84
bagging 155
bootstrapping 155

C

categorical data
  handling 74
  label encoding 78
  one-hot encoding 76
  ordinal encoding 74
centroid 96, 101
cityblock distance 98
classification
  about 123, 139
  dataset, example 140
  logistic regression 143, 146
  model prediction, metrics 141
  multi-class classification 141
  support vector machine (SVM) 146
  tree-based classification 151
clf object 161
clustering concepts 94
clustering methods
  about 102
  density clustering 114
  hierarchical clustering 109
  means separation 105
  spectral clustering 116, 118
coefficient of determination 133
cohesion 101
Conda package manager
  installing 12
convergence 101
correlation coefficient 80, 82
cosine distance 100
cost function 126
cross-validation
  about 38, 157
  multiple validation sets, with k-fold method 159
  validation set 158
curse of dimensionality 79
curved space 99

D

data mining
  about 10
  decisions or predictions, creating 36
  end-to-end example, in Python 25
  Python environments, setting up 11
  readings 10
data sources
  databases 42
  loading, into pandas 41
  types 41
data terminology
  about 21

data types 23
  sample spaces 22
  variable types 22
data types 23
data
  exploring 26
  loading, into memory 25
  plotting 26
  transforming 30, 32, 35
databases
  about 42
  disks 46
  Structured Query Language (SQL) queries 43,
    45
  web sources 46
DBSCAN 114
decision boundary 146
decision tree
  about 151, 152
  node splitting, with Gini 153
dendrogram 109
density clustering 114
depth value 152
derivative 127
derivative descent 128
descriptive analytics 9
dimension reduction
  about 79
  feature selection 79
distance matrix 110
distance metrics 97

E

ensemble learning algorithm 154
estimator API 66
Estimator API 121
Euclidean distance 98
Euclidean space, similarity metrics
  Euclidean distance 98
  manhattan distance 98
  maximum distance 99

F

feature filtering 79, 80
feature scaling

  about 71
  normalization 72
  standardization 73
fit quality regimes 131
forward direction 84
forward sequential selection 84

G

gamma arg 151
gradient 131
gradient descent 123, 125, 131
grid search
  about 38
  for hyperparameter tuning 160
group location, clustering concepts
  about 96
  Euclidean space 96
  non-Euclidean space 97

H

heatmap 82
hierarchical clustering analysis (HCA) algorithm
    111
hierarchical clustering
  about 109
  number of clusters finding, dendrogram reused
    113
  plot dendrogram 114
high bias 131
high variance 131, 136
high-dimensional data 79
High-Performance Computing (HPC) 17
high-performance Python distribution
  installing 17
histograms 56
hyperparameter 37
hyperparameters 124, 157
hypothesis function 125

I

impurity 153
inner arg 29
input data
  categorical data, handling 74
  cleaning 67

feature scaling 71
missing values 67
internal parameters 157
intersection 100

J

Jaccard distance 100
jointplots 58
Jupyter Notebook
launching 15

K

k-fold cross-validation 164
k-fold method 159
k-means algorithm 101
K-means clustering
about 106
k, finding 107
K-means method 109
K-means++ 108
K-means++ 106, 109
kernel trick 150

L

L1 Norm 98
L2 Norm 98
label encoding 74, 78
leaf nodes 152
learning rate 130
level of hierarchy 113
libraries
about 19
installing 18
linear discriminant analysis (LDA) 32
linear regression 134
linkage (l) 110
linkage matrix 110
logistic regression
about 143, 146, 166
regularized logistic regression 146
loss 123
loss function 123, 125

M

manhattan distance 98
marker args 27
mathematical machinery
gradient descent 127, 130
loss function 125
maximum distance 99
mean 24
mean squared error (MSE) 132
means separation
K-means clustering 106
median 24
medioid 96, 97
mini batch 106
missing values
about 67
finding 68
removing 68
replace 70
mode 24
model persistence 166
model
about 123
deploying 166
serialized model, loading 167
serialized model, predicting 167
serializing 167
storing, with pickle module 167
multi-class classification 141
multi-class classification, strategies
one-versus-all 142
one-versus-one 142
multiple folds 159

N

negative correlation 82
nominal 74
non-Euclidean space, similarity metrics
cosine distance 100
Jaccard distance 100
normalization 71, 72
number of clusters 113

O

one-hot encoding 74, 76, 151
one-versus-all 141
one-versus-one 141
ordinal 74
ordinal encoding 74
OrdinalEncoder module 75
out-of-bag (OOB) 155
overfitting 136

P

pairplot 26, 61
palette args 27
pandas
    accessing with 47, 49, 50, 52
    data sources, loading into 41
    sanity checks with 47, 49, 50, 52
    searching with 47, 49, 50, 52
parameter grid 166
Pearson correlation coefficient 24
Pearson's r coefficient 82
penalty arg 146
pickle documentation
    reference link 168
pipeline API 66
pipelined analysis
    about 163
    Scikit-learn's pipeline object 164
plot dendrogram 114
plots
    for data visualization 53
    histograms 56
    jointplots 58
    pairplots 61
    scatter plot 54, 56
    violin plot 59, 61
positive correlation 82
Precision 141
prediction concepts
    about 122
    fit quality regimes 131
    mathematical machinery 125
    prediction nomenclature 124
prediction model

cross-validation 157
    grid search, for hyperparameter tuning 160
    tuning 157
predictive analytics 9
prescriptive analytics 9
principal component analysis (PCA) 30, 71
Pythagorean theorem 98
Python-specific deployment concerns 167
Python
    data mining, end-to-end example 25

R

radius (ε) 114
Random Forest 38
random forest
    about 154
    built-in validation, with bagging 155
    fits, speeding up 155
    overfitting, avoiding 155
Recall 141
recursive feature elimination (RFE) 84
regression 122, 132
regression model
    linear regression 134
    multivariate form, extension 135
    prediction, metric 132
    regression example dataset 133
    regularization, with penalized regression 136
regularization
    about 136
    penalties 137
    with penalized regression 136

S

sample spaces 22
scale-invariant 71
scatter plot 54, 56
Scientific Python Development Environment
    (Spyder) 11
scikit-learn Estimator API 121
scikit-learn transformer API 65
Scikit-learn's pipeline object 164
scikit-learn
    about 65, 121
    reference link 72

Seaborn
  plotting 53
separation
  about 101
  quantifying 35
sequential feature selection 84
sequential version 84
serialization 166
silhouette coefficient (S) 101
silhouette score (Save) 101
similarity matrix 117
similarity metrics 100
similarity metrics, clustering concepts
  about 97
  Euclidean space 98
  non-Euclidean space 99
source node 152
spectral clustering 116, 118
Spyder IDE
  launching 13
standard deviation 24, 133
standardization 71, 73
step function 144
Structured Query Language (SQL) queries 43
Sum squared error (SSE) 111
summary statistics
  about 24
  correlation 24
  locations 24
  shape 24
  spread 24
supervised 86
Support Vector Classifier (SVC) 37
support vector machine (SVM)
  about 37, 146
  kernel trick 150
  soft-margin, with C 150
support vectors 146

T

taxicab metric 98
termination condition, clustering concepts 100
termination condition
  quality score 101
  silhouette score 101
  with number of groupings 101
  without number of groupings 101
tolerance amount 106
transformation 86
transformer API 65
tree-based classification
  about 151
  decision tree 152
  random forest 154
tree-based methods 151
tuning 124, 132

U

union 100
unsupervised 86

V

validation set 157, 158
variable types
  about 22
  dependent variables 22
  independent variables 22
variance 24
variance threshold 80
violin plot 29, 59, 61

W

weak leaner trees 154
web sources
  about 46
  from Scikit-learn 47
  from Seaborn-included sets 47
  from URLs 47
wrapper method 79, 84

www.ingramcontent.com/pod-product-compliance
Lightning Source LLC
Chambersburg PA
CBHW080529060326
40690CB00022B/5076